A COMPANION TO BEDE

A COMPANION TO BEDE

―――⊶◈◈◈⊷―――

A Reader's Commentary on
The Ecclesiastical History of the English People

J. Robert Wright

A Giniger Book
Published in Association with

William B. Eerdmans Publishing Company
Grand Rapids, Michigan / Cambridge, U.K.

© 2008 J. Robert Wright

Published 2008 by
Wm. B. Eerdmans Publishing Co.
2140 Oak Industrial Drive N.E., Grand Rapids, Michigan 49505 /
P.O. Box 163, Cambridge CB3 9PU U.K.
www.eerdmans.com

Published in association with K. S. Giniger Company, Inc., Publishers
1045 Park Avenue, New York, NY 10028

Printed in the United States of America

12 11 10 09 08   7 6 5 4 3 2 1

Library of Congress Cataloging-in-Publication Data

Wright, J. Robert (John Robert), 1936-
A companion to Bede: a reader's commentary on the Ecclesiastical History
of the English people / J. Robert Wright.
p.   cm.
Includes bibliographical references and index.
ISBN 978-0-8028-6309-6 (cloth: alk. paper)
1. Bede, the Venerable, Saint, 673-735. Historia ecclesiastica gentis Anglorum.
2. England — Church history — 449-1066.
3. Church history — Middle Ages, 600-1500.
4. Civilization, Anglo-Saxon.   I. Title.

BR746.W75   2008
274.2′02 — dc22

2008013176

Contents

———❦———

Preface and Acknowledgments

———— ∞∞∞ ————

Bede's *Ecclesiastical History of the English People* is the earliest history of the Anglican tradition of Christianity, written in the early eighth century, and it has been my privilege to teach it for some forty years, both in its Latin original and in its various English translations. My high school Latin teacher back in New Albany, Indiana, Miss Etelka J. Rockenback, first instilled in me a love for the Latin language that enabled me to read it, and that fascination has ever continued with me. The idea of consolidating my notes for students of Bede into a *Companion* that could be published for the use of others was first suggested to me by my good friend, the publisher Kenneth S. Giniger, and I was assisted in the early stages of this process by my student Ben Thomas as well as by ideas and observations gleaned from the literally hundreds of papers that have been written by others who have studied Bede with me over the years. Dr. Milton McC. Gatch, formerly professor of church history and director of the Burke Library, emeritus, at the Union Theological Seminary, was extremely generous in his critical comments that enabled this *Companion* to be more precise on a number of Anglo-Saxon matters, and my gratitude for his expertise in this field I am happy to acknowledge.

My thanks must also be expressed, first to Oxford University Press, and second to Penguin Books Ltd, for their permissions to cite extensively from (and occasionally, to evaluate) the translations of Bede that they have published, as well as to Simon & Schuster for material reproduced at the back of this book. The editorial staff of my own publisher, William B. Eerdmans, have been patient as well as extremely helpful in assisting the transition of this book from manuscript to print and for preparation of the index. Finally, I am grateful to the Dean and Trustees of the General Theological Seminary for their encouragement and for the academic leave from full-time teaching that was necessary in order to accomplish a task of this magnitude.

In concluding this Preface, I also take pause to dedicate this volume to John Andrew and Andrew Mead, the immediate past and present rectors of Saint Thomas Church on Fifth Avenue. There I serve as a priest associate and there, in them, the Anglican tradition finds today one splendid expression of life and worship, albeit one among many, for the twenty-first century that I think the Venerable Bede would no doubt be pleased to praise in his historical narrative. But they in their ministries are now *making* the Church's history, whereas Bede and I, in our books, are merely *writing* it — he the first and greatest, I the least and latest.

J. ROBERT WRIGHT

An Illustration of Bede's Relationship to Eusebius

⸺⊗⊗⊗⸺

Title page of the *Ecclesiastical Histories* of Eusebius and Bede, bound together in one incunabular volume and printed about the year 1500. The earliest printed edition of Bede's *History* is estimated to date from Strasbourg some time between 1474 and 1482 (probably 1475), and at least by 1500 it was being printed again in the same city together with the *Ecclesiastical History* of Eusebius as a single imprint. This fact is attested by the title page of this incunabulum from the Saint Mark's Library of the General Theological Seminary (New York City), Kenneth Cameron collection, dated 1500, formerly in the possession of the Bodleian Library at Oxford. It is recorded as E-129 in Frederick R. Goff, ed., *Incunabula in American Libraries: A Third Census of Fifteenth-Century Books Recorded in North American Collections* (New York: Bibliographical Society of America, 1964), where it is dated 14 March 1550, the printer being Georg Husner of Strasbourg. Some one hundred copies of this imprint are known in various libraries around the world. The title, reproduced here (below), translates as "The Ecclesiastical History of the Divine Eusebius, and the Ecclesiastical History of the English People of the Venerable Bede; together with a summarized annotation of the chapters of each History by their several books." Courtesy Andrew Kadel, Director of the St. Mark's Library.

Ecclesiastica Historia divi Euse-
bii: et Ecclesiastica historia gentis
anglorum venerabilis Bede: cum
vtrarumq3 historiarum per singulos
libros recollecta capitulorum an
notatione.

Map of Anglo-Saxon England, showing dioceses and political divisions.

Introduction

⸺⸺

Just as Eusebius of Caesarea from the early fourth century is generally considered to be "the Founder of Church History," so the Venerable Bede, who seems to have regarded Eusebius as his model, is usually called "the Founder" or "Father" of English Church History. Each of them seems to have regarded the early history of the church, whether generally or in England, as being in one sense a continuation of the story that was begun in the biblical book of the *Acts of the Apostles*. Any early history of the English Church, indeed any early history of England, must draw well over 50 percent of its sources from Bede. It is still a pleasure to read Bede's *History*, both for his observations upon the people of his own time and place, and for the perennial insights he offers which have stood the test of the ages. Although written in Latin, it is regarded as the first important work in the literature of England, as well as the earliest significant history of England, and the first major history of the English Church.

Bede's basic biography is as follows. His year of death was 735, and scholars date the year of his birth as being 672 or 673. He entered the monastery at Wearmouth in the region of Northumbria at the age of seven as an oblate, that is, "offered" or placed there by his kinsmen for education and upbringing, as his autobiographical note at the end of his *History* tells us. Bede remained in the combined monastery of Wearmouth-Jarrow his whole life, taking only short trips to Lindisfarne and York. He was ordained a deacon at the age of nineteen and priest in the year 703 at the age of thirty. Both of these ordinations were performed by John of Beverley, bishop of Hexham, with the blessing of his monastic superior, Ceolfrid. In

1

a touching passage that describes his relatively uneventful life, Bede says "I have spent all my life in this monastery, applying myself entirely to the study of the Scriptures; and, amid the observance of the discipline of the Rule and the daily task of singing in the church, it has always been my delight to learn or to teach or to write." This immediate world in which Bede lived, worked, and prayed can now be visited in person at the Museum of Early Medieval Northumbria at Jarrow, or on the worldwide web at www.bedesworld.co.uk. A nearby place of related interest is the Museum of Antiquities at the University of Newcastle upon Tyne. The Holy Island of Lindisfarne, with its related Exhibition Centre, is also well worth a visit, either in person or on the web at www.Lindisfarne.org.uk.

Bede completed his *Ecclesiastical History of the English People* in 731, shortly before his sixtieth birthday. He also tells us that he wrote just over thirty other books, most of which still survive, which were geared primarily toward the education of his fellow monks. They included a glossary of difficult Latin terms for beginners *(De Orthographia)*, a work on poetic analysis *(De Arte Metrica)*, a basic scientific text *(De Natura Rerum)* that distills much of the work of earlier writers such as Isidore and Pliny, and also a text on the calculation of the correct date of Easter *(De Temporibus)*, which was a subject of obviously fundamental importance because it treated the question of when Christ's resurrection should be celebrated. Bede's interest in the study of time and of dates and of exact chronology comes through clearly in the text of his *Ecclesiastical History,* and he is said to be the first historical writer to incorporate a system of dating by years following the Lord's incarnation *(anno dominicae incarnationis,* or *anno ab incarnatione Domini*), from which the English-speaking world gets its abbreviation A.D. Early examples of such dating can be seen in the first book of his work at the beginnings of chapters 4, 5, and 6.

In addition to these educational pursuits, Bede also wrote a number of more spiritual and theological treatises including a great many commentaries on Scripture, which was his first love. In the list near the end of his *History,* he catalogues them, not in the order in which he wrote them, but in the canonical order of Scripture that he knew. These, in the style of their age, rely heavily on earlier writers, which he knew well, but they also contain some original material from Bede himself. He shows careful attention to the precise biblical text, but, in general, it can be said that he follows the "spiritual" or allegorical, or Alexandrian, method of interpretation, rather than the more literal approach of the school of Antioch.[1] Of particular note among his works on hagiography and biography, Bede also composed two accounts of the life of St. Cuthbert, one in prose and one in verse, which are largely responsible for the widespread following that Cuthbert acquired both in England and on the European continent. Bede's last writing, c. 734 just before his death, a long letter to Bishop Egbert of York that is rather critical of recent happenings, urges that the laity should learn to say the Lord's Prayer and Creed in English, to make the sign of the cross frequently, and to receive Holy Communion at least weekly. Bede's remains are now buried in the Galilee Chapel at Durham Cathedral, which may be seen either in person or on the Durham website. From the ninth century on, he was often called "Venerable," a term that has stayed with him but not a term intended to place him on a level higher than other priests some of whom were also so called.

The extensive popularity of Bede in the Middle Ages is evident from the fact that over 160 medieval manuscript copies of his *History* survive, about half of which are in continental European libraries. There are also over one hundred medieval works that contain extracts from it, nearly all of which are saints' lives. The two earliest manuscripts of Bede's *History* are the "Moore" and "Leningrad" Bedes, both written probably at Wearmouth-Jarrow within a decade after his death and now kept in Cambridge and St. Petersburg, respectively. Some centuries later, the poet Dante in the *Divine Comedy* placed Bede in Canto X of the Paradiso, and in a separate letter reproached the Italian cardinals for neglecting the works of Bede in preference to writings of canon law.[2] The earliest printed edition of Bede's *History* is estimated to come from Strasbourg some time between 1474 and 1482 (probably 1475), and at least by 1500 it was being printed again in the same city together with the *Ec*

---

1. For Bede's approach to Scripture in this way, see his commentaries on Proverbs and the Song of Solomon that are incorporated into the volume of patristic commentaries on the Wisdom literature that I edited for the series *Ancient Christian Commentary on Scripture* [Old Testament IX] (Downers Grove, Ill.: InterVarsity Press, 2005).

2. *The Comedy of Dante Alighieri the Florentine. Cantica III (Il Paradiso)*, trans. Dorothy L. Sayers and Barbara Reynolds (Harmondsworth and Baltimore: Penguin Books, 1962), p. 146 at line 131.

Site of Bede's tomb, Galilee Chapel of Durham Cathedral. Bede's bones were stolen from Jarrow c. 1020 by trickery and carried to Durham Cathedral, where they were first placed in the same tomb with St. Cuthbert (of whom he was the pre-eminent biographer). In 1370 they were enshrined in the Galilee Chapel (named after the Lord's return to Galilee, which at Durham was designated as the final stage in the great processions from the High Altar). Bede's shrine was destroyed at the Reformation, then his bones were re-buried on the same spot, then opened in 1831 and re-interred with this inscription below: *Hac sunt in fossa Bedae venerabilis ossa.* The inscription on the wall behind, added in 1971, is a meditation from Bede's commentary on the Book of Revelation (Apocalypse) 2:28: "Christ is the Morning Star, who when the night of this world is past brings to his saints the promise of the light of life and opens [to them] the everlasting day." *(Photo © Jarrold Publishing and Durham Cathedral, reproduced by kind permission of the publisher.)*

clesiastical History of Eusebius as a single imprint.[3] Bede was proclaimed a "Doctor of the Church" by Pope Leo XIII in 1899, the only Englishman so honored.[4] Today he is commemorated in the liturgical calendars of both the Anglican Communion and the Roman Catholic Church on May 25.

At present, much of the excitement in Bedan studies tends to focus upon the wider picture that can be gleaned from the totality of what Bede wrote, especially his works of biblical exegesis that are becoming more easily accessible, and to view his *History* in that broader perspective. He is no longer being seen merely as a cloistered idealist, but also as a moral reformist and even, by some, as a political activist. The modern reader today is thus being challenged to view him as "a creator, an innovator, and a critic of tradition and of his own age."[5]

How to Use This *Companion*

The purpose of this *Companion* is to assist readers to follow Bede with understanding and insight, and it is recommended that these study-notes be read in tandem with the text itself, ideally chapter by chapter. These notes are not designed for the academic researcher, but for the intelligent and enquiring reader who may desire an extended picture that goes beneath the surface. There will be an inevitable, but not exclusive, attention to ecclesiastical matters, inasmuch as the early history of the church in England is the subject of Bede's work. Ecclesiastical matters may also need more explanation in the world of today, especially as modern editors and commentators sometimes give the impression that Bede's main interests were politics, ge-

3. Incunabulum in the Saint Mark's Library of the General Theological Seminary (New York City), Kenneth Cameron collection, dated 1500. See the illustration in this volume.

4. For the veneration, liturgical commemoration, and subsequent influence of Bede after his death, see chapter 6 of the splendid volume by Sister Benedicta Ward, S.L.G., *The Venerable Bede* (Cistercian Studies series 169; Kalamazoo, Mich.: Cistercian Publications, new edition 1998).

5. Scott DeGregorio, "Introduction: The New Bede," p. 9 of *Innovation and Tradition in the Writings of The Venerable Bede,* ed. Scott DeGregorio (Morgantown: West Virginia University Press, 2006).

ography, and chronology. Official lists of contemporary archbishops and popes, as well as a Table of Events, are provided at the end of this *Companion* for ready reference. Bede's original Latin terms will be mentioned from time to time when they seem to be of wider significance, but in such cases they are also translated.

All quotations of Bede in this *Companion,* unless otherwise noted, are taken from the (latest) "Oxford World's Classics" 1999 paperback reissue of Bede's *Ecclesiastical History of the English People,* edited by Judith McClure and Roger Collins, which is hereby recommended as being the version that is most useful and readily available. Reference will also be made to other translations that illuminate particular points, especially to the latest revised (1990) "Penguin Classics" paperback edition, translated by Leo Sherley-Price and revised by R. E. Latham, with new introduction and notes by D. H. Farmer, so that this *Companion* can be easily used by readers of either the Oxford or Penguin editions. Attention is also drawn to the remarks on Anglo-Saxon political history and geography at the beginning of the Oxford edition as well as the useful map there. Other maps and genealogies of rulers are found at the end of the Penguin edition, although its details and spellings are not always the same as those given in the Oxford. Identifications of persons and places already given in the endnotes to the Oxford edition will generally not be repeated here. The Oxford translation, it should be noted, corresponds to the critical text that was edited in Latin and translated into English by Bertram Colgrave and R. A. B. Mynors in the Oxford Medieval Texts series (Oxford: Clarendon, 1969).

Readers are cautioned against the confusion that may come from attempting to use earlier Penguin editions, where for example the Latin words that appear quite frequently in the Colgrave and Mynors Latin text of 1969, *Scotti, Scottos, Scottia, Scottorum,* were regularly translated as "Scots," "Scotland," and "Scottish" in earlier Penguin editions but now in the Penguin text are translated as "Irish," "Ireland," and so on, as they have been also in the Oxford text since 1969, without any explanation being given in the later Penguin editions of the reason for the shift from "Scots" to "Irish." The latest Penguin edition (1990, p. 361) admits that "Bede's word *Scotti* is translated 'Irish' throughout," but does not say why the change was made, whereas the Oxford text of Colgrave and Mynors at its first publication in 1969 (p. 16, n. 1) noted that "*Scotti* in Bede always means the Irish race whether in Scotland or Ireland. *Scottia* refers to Ireland alone though he uses *Hibernia* too, apparently using both terms indiscriminately as in the first paragraph of iv. 26."

A complete English text of Bede's *History*, although copied from an older translation dated from 1903/1910 (and containing some errors), is also available online by means of the "Internet Medieval Source Book," and located at www.fordham.edu/halsall/basis/Bede.

Procedural Suggestion

Read a chapter of Bede, then read the notes for that chapter in this *Companion,* then go back and reread the text of that chapter in Bede himself. But do not read the *Companion* without also reading Bede himself!

Brief Overview

At the risk of anticipating some phraseology that will be used again later in this *Companion,* it can be said in a general way that Bede seems to have two major purposes in writing his *History* (as well as several minor themes that will be considered not here but later as we pass through his individual books and chapters). First of all, he is desirous of writing *The Ecclesiastical History of the English People* just as his title indicates, and this involves such concerns as chronological development, comprehensive treatment, fairness, accuracy, and attention to sources and to details that have usually been the objective goals and characteristics of good historians, but always under the subjective influence of his own perspectives and within the limitations under which he worked. His second major purpose is to relate the gradual movement of the peoples of his land from diversity to unity that he sees reflected in the decision for the Roman tradition of Christianity over the Celtic one, including the Roman way for calculating the date of Easter, that was made at the Synod of Whitby in the year 664. Bede had been born only a few years after that synod, and still by the time that he was completing his

History in 731 there remained many traces of Celtic individualism that, to his orderly mind, militated against God's unitary purpose and intended destiny for the land and its people.

The dating of Easter was the most prominent manifestation of this concern for the primacy of Roman over Celtic, for it was the point of origin for the whole liturgical calendar, the moment of resurrection when heaven breaks into earth and time crosses with eternity, and was thus directly linked to the observance of the central feast of the Christian year. When Bede records the spread of Celtic Christianity in Northumbria one can already sense the tension in his hand as he writes, for he is quite certain that Roman Christianity is the true expression of the Christian faith at the same time that he also admires greatly the asceticism and spirituality of such Celtic figures as Columba and Aidan who, in his words, had a genuine "zeal for God though not entirely according to knowledge" (cf. III.3).

Theology and politics are always interfaced in Bede's *History,* and it has been remarked that the way to an effective unification of the Celtic and Roman strands, once the threat of paganism was diminished, really became possible after the victory of Oswiu over Penda at the battle of the Winwood River in 654-55. As Bede saw things, there had long been much chaos and confusion, with Celtic monks and bishops still observing Celtic rites and the wrong date of Easter, thus placing themselves, in effect, out of communion with the See of Canterbury, which observed the Roman rites and kept the one true date of Easter. (The discrepancy also meant different dates for the Ascension and Pentecost as well.) This state of affairs had even gotten to the point, he says, that "it sometimes happened that Easter was celebrated twice in the same year, so that the king had finished the fast and was keeping [Celtic] Easter Sunday, while the queen and her people were still in Lent and observing [Roman] Palm Sunday"! This same care for order can be seen, likewise, as Bede carefully records the succession-lists of bishops in order of consecration, obviously stemming from the Roman sense of order and centralized authority.

The debates at Whitby were conducted between Colman, bishop and abbot of Lindisfarne, representing the Celtic tradition that had come by way of Iona and Ireland from the north, and Wilfrid, abbot of Ripon and later archbishop of York, representing the Roman tradition of Christianity that had come from the southeast by means of St. Augustine, who had been sent to England by Pope Gregory the Great. The debates at Whitby focused upon the correct calculation for the date of Easter and the correct form of clerical tonsure, the underlying question being whether the kingdom was to continue to follow the divergent Celtic ways or to be united under an allegiance to the Church of Rome. The Celtic argument, upheld by Colman and supported by Abbess Hilda and her community, focused on antiquity, individual choice, and decentralized authority, whereas the Roman argument, championed by Wilfrid, called for universality, discipline, and an understanding of doctrinal development under centralized, international leadership. Here at the Synod of Whitby the triumph of Roman Christianity over Celtic was sealed as the English Church was formally united by the decision of King Oswiu of Northumbria in favor of Rome. The political factors that had brought him to power also made possible this firm decision. Bede understandably makes this event, this synod, the pivotal turningpoint of his entire *History,* placing it towards the end of the third of his five books and just in the center, although it is possible that the lines between "Celt" and "Roman" were not as finely drawn as his account suggests.

Was the decision of Whitby a mistake, a sellout to size and organization, to political power and ecclesiastical order, over the things of the Spirit? There is no ambiguity in Bede's remarks, for to prefer the teaching of the Celtic fathers, "a handful of people in one corner of the remotest of islands," over "the universal Church of Christ which is spread throughout the world," even though he sincerely admired the simplicity and poverty and individual examples of holiness seen in the Celts, would be to relegate England to a continued existence in an ecclesiastical backwater. Towards the end of his fifth and final book, after summarizing the biblical, chronological, historical, and theological reasons that underlie the Roman position on the Easter controversy, Bede tells us with some relief that in the year 716 the island and community of Iona finally accepted the decision of Whitby in favor of the Roman dating for Easter and the Roman form of the tonsure. Of course the controversy was never finally settled, as we shall see, and many other themes are considered in passing.

J. Robert Wright

A Companion to Bede

—— ⌒∞⌒ ——

Preface

This and the concluding synopsis (at the end of Book V.24) provide almost all we know of Bede's life. From beginning to end, "servant of Christ and priest" *(famulus Christi et presbyter)* is how he describes himself at both these locations in the text. In his Preface Bede gives us an insight into his methodology and the reasons why he is writing an *Ecclesiastical History of the English People*. Ceolwulf was a king of Northumbria from 729 to 737, after which he became a monk of Lindisfarne. It is interesting to note that kings are almost the only lay people (not clergy and not monks) whom Bede mentions. His deference to royalty can be seen in the first line, where Bede reveals that the Preface was written after the *History* itself was finished and for the benefit of none other than the same Ceolwulf. Bede's title, *Historia Ecclesiastica Gentis Anglorum* is sometimes translated into English as "History of the Church in England" but the Latin title, when translated literally, "The Ecclesiastical History of the English People" reveals a broader scope. Bede had already sent the king his first draft, but now, ready for general copying, he sends along his completed text.

In the Preface Bede goes on to say that his intention is to "tell of good men and their good estate" (Penguin: "record good things of good men"), so that "the thoughtful listener is spurred on to imitate the good" or, conversely, to "record the evil ends of wicked men" so that readers will be encouraged "to eschew what is harmful and perverse." Here Bede combines the "great men" theory of history with a distinctly moral purpose. In addition to these classical themes from the field of historiography, Bede also shows a notable and quite contemporary concern for accurate reporting of sources, although he would be the first to say that he is not writing "modern critical history," with an attempt to be objectively value-free in the same way that "history" is understood today. A distance of well over 1300 years separates him from our own day, and we must not pretend otherwise.

The influence of Canterbury on Bede is clear from the lengthy praise he bestows upon the abbot Albinus. Albinus, the Preface notes, was Bede's "principal authority and helper." We know from other sources that Albinus was abbot of the monastery of Saints Peter and Paul (later, St. Augustine's), Canterbury, from around 709-732, in succession to Hadrian. Albinus's credentials include his studies under notable ecclesiastical figures, but of special interest is Albinus's reliance on the memory of a certain assistant named Nothhelm. Here an explanation for Bede's preeminence among the earliest English historians is appropriate. Bede did not merely collect information from both written and oral sources, but by his own claim he has purposefully striven for accuracy and he cites his authorities for all to see. Nothhelm himself became archbishop of Canterbury, 735-739, shortly after Bede's *Ecclesiastical History* was completed and just as Bede was dying. Nothhelm, like Bede, was a scholar as Bede attests in the Preface where he notes that Nothhelm's memories, whether given to Bede in written or oral format, derived from Nothhelm's own search of the papal archives with papal permission.

One final consideration from the Preface is Bede's closing rationale for the methodology he has followed, which provides further clues about Bede's reliability as a historian and the premises upon which he operates. We note his reference to "the principles of true history" *(vera lex historiae),* a phrase that he borrowed from the Latin of St. Jerome and had used earlier in his commentary on the Gospel of St. Luke. In this phrase, at the end of his comments about the acquisition of his materials on St. Cuthbert, Bede carefully asserts two things. The first is that he is giving allegiance to a superior historiographical principle, namely, "the principles of true history," but also that he believes that such laws have come down from higher authority. This invites reflection upon our own notions of value-free objectivity, as Bede does say that he took his information either from written sources or from the "trustworthy testimony of reliable witnesses," whom he often names. By leaving his claims of veracity open to challenge in this way, Bede reveals a strikingly modern stance and essentially invites anyone who would know the truth to read his work critically and continue to investigate any topic they may question with a firm belief that the truth will be revealed to diligent seekers. Yet he also begs for the prayers of his readers, a request that a modern historian today would be less likely to ask.

Book I.1

In this first book, Bede sets out to describe what he sees as the most salient features of British geography, the earliest contacts with Rome, and the very early beginnings of Christianity in Britain. He begins by listing a few of the physical and economic factors that to him seem to indicate the overall agreeableness of the British Isles. "Albion" is the classical and literary name for Britain, probably derived from the Latin adjective *albus* that means "white" and thus related to the chalk-white cliffs along the southern coast. Situated as it is at the very terminus of the Roman Empire, Bede's description of pre-Roman Britain implies an ideal place of near-perfection. It is "rich in crops and in trees, and has good pasturage for cattle and beasts of burden. It also produces vines in certain districts, and has plenty of both land- and waterfowl of various kinds." Bede goes on to note a variety of other useful and pleasant features ranging from the abundance of rivers and fish, the presence of copper, iron, lead, silver, and jet which is glossy black, as well as the possibility of health resorts where men and women can take in the hot waters, being separated for the sake of modesty into separate areas.

This section continues with Bede's curious observation that the four races and five languages of England are in accordance with the example of the Pentateuch of the Old Testament, "just as the divine law is written in five books." This numerical analogy sheds light on the praise that Bede has already heaped on the natural abundance of the region by also indicating a theological reason for his preference of England. The comment on language is particularly telling as Bede goes on to include a language that is particular to no single ethnic group in his list of important languages of the region. That is, the first four languages that Bede lists are coupled to their respective ethnic groups — to the English, British, Irish, and Pictish peoples. The fifth, however, which allows the happy numerological agreement with the Pentateuch, is Latin, which also just happens to be the language of the church. It is the language that Bede sees as capable of uniting these disparate peoples through their study of the Bible in the context of the church's liturgy, and of course it is the language in which he writes.

Furthermore, it seems significant that none of the people in this geographical survey are truly native to the land, at least according to Bede's reckoning. At some point, each group has arrived by boat from some other country as if drawn by some invisible attraction to this blessed land. The curious story of the Picts who arrived as a male-only expedition and needed wives may have been included as a background story to explain some of the regional political difficulties, described in Book I.12, of the newer settlers of the southern portions of England made up principally of Anglo-Saxons and Britons and the older settlers located in modern Scotland and Ireland, who were predominantly Irish and Pictish.

Book I.2-3

The Roman occupation of Britain and the ascendance of Christianity in Britain are the subjects of chapters 2-34 of Book I. Bede begins this era in I.2 with the arrival of the first Romans in Britain under the leadership of Julius Caesar. In this chapter, Bede's information comes almost entirely from the work of the fifth-century Spanish priest Orosius, *Historia adversus Paganos,* written 417-418 (Bede's dating is a bit off), which had emphasized the role of divine providence in history. Bede's sense of national destiny in salvation history thus begins to be shown very early on. The conquests of successive Roman emperors, in Bede's view, are marked by frequent setbacks. Julius Caesar and Claudius, the two emperors whom Bede has singled out for special comment in these chapters, are both presented in fairly bland terms. This is no doubt owing in some part to Bede's heavy reliance on other sources, but is also related to Bede's overarching theme of national destiny. The pagan emperors are often beset with personal political difficulties, Julius Caesar with actual tempests at sea and Claudius with political storms throughout his empire.

Book I.4

King Lucius makes his appeal to Pope Eleutherius to be made a Christian. The Pope, whose name is related to the Greek word for "freedom," happily grants the king's pious request, which marks the beginning of the new freedom in Christ which Bede sees spreading over the English countryside.

While Bede's facts are not in line with this particular legend of sixth-century origin, they are at least not of his own invention. This particular story derives from an error in the source known as *Liber Pontificalis*. "Eleutherius"[1] was not Pope until c. 175-189. Lucius was not a British king, but was really Abgar IX, King of Edessa c. 206-216. This and other legends, however, were invented to explain a true fact, that Christianity seems to have somehow reached Britain by the late second century, probably by commercial and military contacts between Britain and Gaul. Of further interest regarding this particular legend is the mention of this event later in Book V.24, where Bede dates the conversion of Lucius at 167 instead of 156, indicating the possibility of multiple sources. The story of the rebuilding of Hadrian's Wall by the Emperor Septimius Severus in 205-208 continues to follow Bede's chief source for this period, the Spanish priest and historian Orosius. As with the legend of King Lucius, first Orosius and then Bede, because of him, mistakenly believe that Severus was the original builder of the wall. The wall was actually built in the early part of the second century under the Emperor Hadrian, who ruled from 117 to 138.

Book I.6

Like the preceding four chapters, chapter 6 relies heavily on material from Orosius. The Great Persecution in which Diocletian "ordered the churches to be laid waste and the Christians persecuted and slain," took place in the period from 303 to 311. Bede lists this persecution as the "tenth persecution after Nero," which while not strictly incorrect is nevertheless confusing.

---

1. So-called "official" lists of Popes vary in spelling his name either "Eleutherius" or "Eleutherus."

Like the counting of the Roman emperors, the number of persecutions is always subject to revision, often to support some angular theological or exegetical purpose. So, while Bede counts the persecution of Diocletian as the tenth persecution to follow Nero's efforts against Christians in Rome, the number does depend upon how one counts them. Bede's final words at the end of I.6 bring to a close his prehistory of England and anticipate a noble theme to which he will return often before the end of his work: "In fact Britain also attained to the great glory of bearing faithful witness to God."

Book I.7

Bede introduces the martyrdom of St. Alban with a poetic fragment from another ecclesiastical source, the Italian poet and priest Venantius Fortunatus, who became bishop of Poitiers in the late sixth century after composing the work that Bede cites, *Praise of the Virgins*. Fortunatus had noted in his book that "in fertile Britain's land was noble Alban born" (as the Penguin translation renders it), which serves to validate Bede's high view of the island while also establishing the birthplace of Alban. The birthplace no one seems to have disputed, so we can safely infer that Bede's primary intention was to observe the blessed state of England rather than to certify a location for Alban's origin.

Alban's martyrdom is recorded as occurring on June 22, and this day is reserved for his commemoration in the liturgical calendars of many churches that remember him as the proto-martyr of Britain. As for the year of his death, it had been generally thought that his martyrdom happened during the Great Persecution under Diocletian, some time between 301 and 305, but this conjecture has largely been rejected. Recently, there has come to light some good evidence to suggest that Alban's martyrdom may go back even into the reign of Septimius Severus 193-211, probably in 209 AD. Alban gave shelter to a Christian priest fleeing from persecution, then was converted by the priest while giving him shelter. Alban gave himself up, dressed in the cloak of the priest, and was martyred instead of the priest, on the hill where the abbey (now cathedral) church of St. Alban stands. Subsequent tradition has called this priest St. Amphibalus, a name which itself means "cloak." Although the evidence here in Bede dates this to 22 June and points to the year 303-4, in 1968 John Morris presented initially convincing (although subsequently questioned) evidence to move this date back to 22 June 209, under the persecution of Septimius Severus, and to this we now turn.

Morris bases his conclusions[2] upon earlier manuscripts now available, especially one from Turin around the eighth or ninth century, which was copied from an original dated to about the year 500 but not known to Bede. The Turin manuscript reads: "Alban received a fugitive cleric and put on his garment and his cloak *(habitu et caracalla)* that he was wearing and delivered himself up to be killed instead of the priest. . . . and was delivered immediately to the evil Caesar Severus." Now it happens that "Caracalla" was the nickname of the Emperor Severus's son and co-ruler Antoninus, who was called "Caracalla" because of the great cloak *(caracalla)* that he customarily wore, and Morris holds it likely that an earlier version of the Turin manuscript carried a marginal note *et Caracalla* beside the line with the name of Severus and was thus intended to indicate that he was delivered up to both Severus and Caracalla. In turn, the Turin copyist, knowing that *caracalla* was the name for a cloak but not that it was the nickname of the co-ruler Antoninus, inserted it into the wrong place in the text, assuming that it was intended to supplement the description of the garment *(habitu)* that Alban had put on! Later still, when the word *caracalla* in Latin became obsolete for "cloak" and was superseded by the word *amphibalon, caracalla* in the text was replaced by *amphibalon,* and readers (such as the chronicler Geoffrey of Monmouth in the twelfth century) then began to interpret the latter word as meaning a person, the name of the priest, rather than a supplementary description of the garment! Hence the priest came to be named Amphibalus. And the final step in this process was the alleged discovery, or "invention" (from the Latin verb *invenio,* which means "to find") of the

2. John Morris, "The Date of Saint Alban," *Hertfordshire Archaeology,* vol. 1 (1968); Arthur Swinson, *The Quest for Alban* (Fraternity of the Friends of St. Albans Abbey, 1971). For the questions, see Richard Sharpe, pp. 114-18 of Alan Thacker and Richard Sharpe, eds., *Local Saints and Local Churches in the Early Medieval West* (Oxford: Oxford University Press, 2002); in the handlist compiled by John Blair at the end of this volume, however, Alban's martyrdom is dated as "probably 3rd cent." (p. 510).

supposed relics of this priest around the same time near the same spot, and the erection of a separate shrine dedicated to him to contain them.

The account of Alban's martyrdom sheds considerable light on a number of early medieval conventions regarding the relationship of Christian and pagan rites and how they are expressed by Christian writers. For example, Bede's description of the interview in which Alban confesses his devotion to Christ records that "The judge was standing before the devils' altars and offering sacrifices to them." For the word "altar" here, Bede follows the general practice of most Christian Latin writers in using the Latin word *ara* to designate a heathen altar, as he also does in II.13 ("the altars and shrines of the idols") and III.30 ("they either abandoned or destroyed the temples and altars they had erected"). But when Christian authors write to designate the altar of the One True God they generally choose a different word, the Latin *altare*. Bede follows this conventional distinction throughout the rest of his *History,* and there are other examples to be found at I.15, 29, 30, II.13, 14, 15, III.2, 17, 19, IV.13, and V.10, 16, 19, 20, 21. In all of these references the word *altare* indicates the existence of a Christian altar, the lone exception being a quotation that occurs in II.13. Here Bede does use *altare* to designate a heathen altar, but from the mouth of a heathen priest who is speaking: "I advise your Majesty that we should promptly abandon and commit to the flames the temples and the altars which we have held sacred without reaping any benefit." Presumably, this aberration is allowed in the case of a direct quotation.

Another interesting example of Bede's use of language can be found in Alban's reply to the judge when he was asked about his familial and racial ties. Alban's reply, "Know that I am now a Christian, and am ready to do a Christian's duty," can carry a spectrum of meanings, depending upon how one translates *Christianisque officiis vacare,* the last half of the sentence, where the Penguin version, by contrast, reads "and carry out Christian rites." The difficulty for translators comes with the verb *vacare,* which has the primary meaning "to be free," "to be empty," or "to be absent from," but can carry further meanings by extension such as "to have time for" or "to attend" or "to devote oneself to." While the Oxford translation suggests the total range of obligations in the Christian moral and civic life, the connotation of the Penguin translation tends to convey an almost sacramental devotion. Whichever, the phrase obviously underscores Alban's already bold statement of his faith and implies that Alban is not merely a nominal Christian but a faithful and active one. On a different note, this reply from Alban when asked about his family and race also hearkens back to Bede's implication in I.1 that not only five languages but also five races exist in England. In I.1 Bede only included Latin as a language, but here "Christian" is the self-proclaimed identification of the proto-martyr of Britain.

There is also a close parallel between the miracles performed by Alban and the miracles reported in the Old Testament. Alban's transit over a rushing river on dry land looks much like the crossing of the Red Sea (Exodus 14) or the Jordan River (Joshua 3). Unfortunately for Alban, his desire to hasten his execution and subsequent entrance into heaven was not immediately successful. By Alban's avoiding a crowded bridge in a miraculous fashion, the would-be executioner saw the power of Alban's faith and was converted on the spot, after which a new executioner had to be summoned not only for Alban but for the recent convert as well! The second miracle, a spring emerging at Alban's feet to provide for his final earthly comfort, hails from the story in Exodus 17, where a miraculous provision of water in a time of need occurs for Moses. The other martyrs whom Bede mentions almost in passing at the end of this chapter, Aaron and Julius, have been taken from an earlier writer named Gildas, and little else is known of them.

Book I.8

Bede's offhand references to Christians in England in the late second or early third century are quite tantalizing. These references may indicate the existence of very early, rather advanced, pre-Anglo-Saxon liturgy and worship in Britain and may imply at least the possibility of a very early Celtic Christian presence or influence. In contrast to his treatment of the later, non-Roman Christian expressions of piety, Bede does not censure these early Christians for their non-conformity. He does, however, note that they were misled by the Arian heresy ("madness," says Bede), which denied the divinity of Christ, a controversy that raged throughout the Christian world in the early fourth century and was one of the major reasons necessitating the first ecumenical council, which was held at Nicaea in 325. Bede, borrowing from the sixth-century British monk and historian Gildas, does remark upon Britain as "an island which always delights in hearing something new and holds firmly to no sure belief" — an insight into the English temperament, for better or worse, that has remained as widely held even up to the present. The mention of Constantius here refers to the Emperor Constantius Chlorus, who died at York in 306, and was the father of the great emperor Constantine (cf. Eusebius, *Ecclesiastical History* VIII.13).

Book I.9-10

While the contents of chapter 9 are taken almost entirely from Orosius, chapter 10 introduces a recurring problem in the spread of Christianity in England, namely the threat, real or perceived, of Pelagianism. This belief, later named a heresy, actually maintained that human beings, strictly by their own ability and apart from the grace of God, could take action leading to their own salvation. This deviant theological assertion was the work of a writer named Pelagius. Of British extraction, Pelagius was teaching in Rome near the end of the fourth and into the early fifth century. The great St. Augustine of Hippo is the best remembered of those who expended their energies in the refutation of Pelagius. Pelagius himself seems to have accepted his defeat and disappears, along with most of his writings, from the pages of history, although a number of other theologians continued to spread his doctrine even after it had been declared a heresy by Pope Innocent I. "The rhetorician" here is St. Prosper of Aquitaine, who was sent by St. Augustine to St. Jerome during this controversy and later exercised a quiet but considerable influence and is remembered today especially as the one who enunciated the principle, "The rule of prayer establishes the rule of faith," which became known by the Latin tag *Lex orandi lex credendi*. Orosius, we may note, was strongly anti-Pelagian.

Book I.11-16

Chapter 11 continues Bede's dependence upon Orosius, its final paragraph being Bede's own contribution as background to two items of considerable interest. The first is Bede's clear espousal of a retribution dogma in I.14. Here, at the end of the various invasions and repulsions set forth in chapters 11-13, the Britons finally drive the invaders from their soil. Unfortunately, their happiness is short-lived after their victory, for the blessing that arises from driving out the pagan invaders is rich but dangerous in its own right: "There was so great an abundance of corn in the island as had never before been known. [However, with] this affluence came an increase of luxury." Bede goes on to record what he seems to see as the likely result of such material prosperity, particularly in the absence of a strong and unified spiritual life. Indeed, this abundance was "followed by every kind of foul crime; in particular, cruelty and hatred of the truth and love of lying increased, so that if anyone appeared to be milder than the rest and somewhat more inclined to the truth, the rest, without consideration, rained execrations and missiles upon him as if he had been an enemy of Britain." Of course, such general rebellion against goodness was not likely to escape the notice of divine justice and hence, a "virulent plague suddenly fell upon these corrupt people." As Bede continues his tale, the divine retribution is thus unfolded, and the impious and greatly weakened Britons look (with the advice of their secular king) to the Anglo-Saxons for help in keeping out the Irish and the Picts. The result of the Britons' appeal is finally to make their matters worse until finally the Britons put the Angles to flight at the battle of Mount Badon. This battle occurred in or shortly before the year 500. Bede carefully notes two changes in the Britons' strategy, to which he attributes their success: prayer and Roman leadership, which are among his characteristic emphases.

Initially puzzling in these chapters and throughout Bede's *History* is the complete omission of St. Patrick, for which three equally plausible explanations present themselves. The first is that Bede is writing about the church in England, by which he obviously intends Anglo-Saxon England, and not primarily about the church in Ireland, Scotland, or Wales, which may also help to explain the omission of St. David. Second, Bede may not have been sufficiently convinced of the historical accuracy or importance of many of the legends that were in circulation about Patrick. The dispute surrounding the date of Patrick's birth goes back as early as the seventh century. In the face of conflicting reports about a figure who could be omitted without offending the British audience for whom Bede was presumably writing, Bede may have decided that silence was better than public uncertainty. Another equally compelling possibility presents itself in the light of Bede's reservations about the non-conforming Irish clergy, reservations that become readily apparent in Book II of his *Ecclesiastical History* and may have been strong enough to convince Bede that he should omit mention of Patrick for fear of sending a message of ambiguity. By the time Bede was writing, Patrick may have been so highly regarded that to include him in a history that looks mainly to Canterbury and Rome for theological inspiration and allegiance might have made Bede's pro-Roman views less clear or convincing. Whatever the case, it is impossible to believe that Bede had never heard of Patrick, and therefore, we must assume that the omission was a deliberate editorial choice on Bede's part, regardless of the underlying reasons and no matter how much today we regret it for whatever reason.

Book I.17-19

Much of what Bede records here follows the life of St. Germanus, written about 475 by Constantius of Lyons. Germanus, who died in the 440s, was bishop of Auxerre. As with the other miracles mentioned, Bede has brought to light the wonders performed by Germanus in the name of Christ which have close biblical analogies. The stilling of the storm in I.17 fits nicely with Matthew 8:23-27, while the healing of the blind is ubiquitous in the gospels, particularly as a sign of the coming kingdom of God. (See Matthew 11:5.) Bede's own belief about the purpose of miracles is easily deduced from his concluding note that follows the one miracle account in these chapters, at the end of I.18: "After these incidents, a countless number of men turned to the Lord on the same day."

For Bede, it would seem as though signs and miracles are an appropriate phenomenon in his place and era, if not actually a substitute for the persecution and martyrdom that permeated so much of the early church in the era before the reign of Constantine. In both cases, they are seen to attest God's power at work within the process of human history, whether verifying a person's holiness, or indicating the truth of their witness, or reinforcing the faith of others. Bede's miracle stories, we note, are generally included within his *History* for the purpose of explaining *why* things happened, rather than *how* they happened, for the latter is usually of less interest to him. That is, he usually seeks to go beyond the simple historical account, in order to give a theological explanation for the historical facts that he has recorded.

Book I.20

While the roles of bishops and generals have grown steadily further from each other in the modern period of history, the leadership of bishops in battle in Bede's day was certainly not unheard of. "With such apostolic leaders," Bede says, "it was Christ Himself who fought in their camp." The general conception of spirituality in this era seems to be quite activist in its character, and the charism of military leadership both a cause and an effect of the close connection of sacred and secular at that time, which enables him also to establish early in his *History* the legitimacy and authority of the office of bishop. Bede's own sense of national destiny seems to confirm this observation. Remnants of early Christian pacifism emerge in this account, however, which differs remarkably from its close biblical parallel found in the book of Judges 7:15-23. In the account of Gideon's victory over the Midianites in that book, there is seemingly no foe left unslain. By contrast, here in Bede's account of "the Alleluia victory" over the Saxons and Picts, the British victors are restrained in their innocence and are mere observers of God's provision as they shout the "Alleluia" that is characteristic of the Easter season they have just entered. Bede concludes: "The bishops thus overcame the enemy without the shedding of blood; they won a victory by faith and not by might."

In addition to the very indistinct line between the sacred and secular as observed in the behavior of Bishops Germanus and Lupus, Bede's narration of the military proceedings contains a number of fascinating traces of ecclesiastical customs. Of these, some, like daily instruction during Lent, have disappeared on a daily basis from the catholic tradition in the West. Others such as baptism on the eve of Easter have endured or have even been restored in many churches' traditions. One final trace from the end of the battle is the practice of the loud and threefold "Alleluia," prominent, as Bede was aware, in the Roman liturgy for Easter. The troops, who had been undergoing catechetical instruction throughout Lent and then were just recently baptized during the liturgy of the Easter Vigil, now came to this battle with all this on their mind, and so it seems quite reasonable to assume that they were inspired verbally by this practice. In many Christian churches of the West the same tradition of singing a triple "alleluia" on Easter eve is still observed and in others it has been restored in recent decades.

Book I.21-22

These chapters bring to an end Bede's story of the uncertain oscillation between the catholic faith and the Pelagian heresy and a number of other questionable doctrines that had plagued the land for some time. The "Severus" who is mentioned at the beginning of this chapter may have become bishop of Vence (province of Arles) rather than bishop of Trier.

In the healing of Elafius's son, the role of miracles in witness to the true faith is again asserted. When Elafius arrives together with his whole tribe, Germanus quickly ascertains the texture of the catholicity of their faith and determines that by and large the people remain loyal. From the witness of the healing of the boy's leg, Bede records that "the catholic faith, already implanted in the hearts of them all, was further strengthened." Germanus having gone to Italy on a mission of diplomacy for the British Christians and dying in Rome, Bede's turn of phrase to describe Germanus's death is quite poetic. The Latin states that Germanus *"migravit ad Christum,"* that is, "he departed to be with Christ."

Despite this hopeful series of events and Germanus's happy departure, Britain could not long persevere in the faith without a true shepherd (who, we soon learn, will be St. Augustine). True to biblical form, a generation arose that did not remember their past history. The Britons are guilty of all sorts of things, but worst of all is their failure to preach to their former enemies, the Angles and Saxons. This chapter and the next bring to a close the introductory section of Bede's *History* and mark the end of his closest reliance on earlier historians. Chapter 22 ends with a restatement of a significant theme for Bede: "Nevertheless God in his goodness did not reject the people whom He foreknew, but He had appointed much worthier heralds of the truth to bring this people to the faith." Bede's suggestion of predestination, or divine foreknowledge, implied in this remark will be commented upon in II.14 below, but already at the end of I.22 we are alerted to the fact that divine agency, a category that is of course absent from modern historical writing, will be very much a part of the substance of Bede's narrative. It has been calculated that *Deus* ("God") occurs in some 313 passages spread across 98 of his 140 chapters, and *Christus* in 172 passages spread across 65 chapters.[3]

Book I.23

Now we come to the beginnings of Bede's own work, properly speaking. The Gregorian mission under St. Augustine was dispatched from Rome by Pope St. Gregory the Great in 596. It did not arrive in England until 597. The story of this mission has much in common with the evangelical fervor displayed by Bede in earlier chapters. It was in fact the first papal mission to a pagan people. Here, for Bede, is the main line of Christian history. As such he reveals a somewhat millenarian view of Augustine and his mission. Bede's view does not appear to be millenarian in the fundamentalistic sense of a particular and exact working out of something deduced from Scripture, but, rather, Bede's more moderate view seems to be more along the lines that God has chosen Augustine as the appointed emissary of the gospel to the island, and that Augustine's works would usher in a new Christian era in Britain. Augustine had been a prefect of Pope Gregory's own monastery, St. Andrew's on the Caelian Hill in Rome. Gregory was abbot of this monastery from 585 to 590. Because of this prior association, Augustine owed a certain obedience and fidelity to Gregory. By virtue of these monastic attachments, Augustine was someone whom Gregory felt could be relied upon. His reliability would at first seem to be questionable, but Augustine's deference to Gregory appears to be strong enough to make up where his courage was wanting.

3. N. J. Higham, *(Re-)Reading Bede* (New York: Routledge, 2006), p. 149.

Pope Gregory in writing to Augustine refers to himself as *Servus Servorum Dei,* the "servant of the servants of God." Gregory the Great was the first Pope to use this title, and it was he who rebuked the Patriarch of Constantinople for claiming the title "universal bishop" ("Ecumenical Patriarch"). Gregory's humble spirit, or at least the humble title, was later eclipsed by a successor, Gregory VII, who would eventually claim for himself in the late eleventh century the same "universal" title that Gregory the Great had so notably rejected. We must also note the literary style of majesty and superiority in Pope Gregory's letters here and later. Generally this style had been a feature of papal correspondence ever since the time of Pope Damasus I (366-84), who became the first Roman bishop to use the majestic plural ("We"), the first bishop of Rome to appropriate the title "apostolic" to the Roman see, and the first Roman bishop to address other bishops as "sons." (Not always was this latter practice followed, however, and sometimes subsequent Popes wrote to other bishops as "brother," as can be seen in the letters of Boniface V in II.8 and of Honorius I in II.18.)

The "indiction" which Gregory mentions at the end of this letter in chapter 23 is a cycle of fifteen years, used originally for computing land-tax and then for reckoning time. Dating by indiction originated under the Roman ruler Licinius in 312 AD and later came to be added to dates of imperial and consular years. Dating according to indiction years, however, was not a straightforward matter. The number of an indiction (such as here, the fourteenth indiction) really only indicates the place that a given year occupies in an unspecified cycle of fifteen years. This was computed by subtracting 312 from the actual year of grace (the year *anno domini*) and then dividing by fifteen, the remainder being the number of the year in a given cycle (indiction) of fifteen. If the remainder is 0, of course, the number of the indiction year is fifteen. And the quotient, in such a computation, is one less than the actual number of the indiction (i.e., the quotient plus one indicates in which fifteen-year cycle after 312 the given year falls). Thus, the letter of Pope Gregory here in chapter 23 is dated "the fourteenth indiction": 596-312 = 284 divided by 15 = 18 quotient plus a remainder of 14, which confirms a date during the fourteenth year during the nineteenth indiction (or nineteenth fifteen-year cycle after 312, i.e., the period 582-597 AD, in this case 596). Dating by indiction continued to be used by the papacy and various chanceries in both Eastern and Western Europe in the early Middle Ages, but by the thirteenth century it had generally been discarded except in formal notarial instruments. The foregoing explanation does not, of course, take into account the many different days when indiction-years were thought to begin in various medieval systems of reckoning. To cite only two examples: In the Eastern Empire the indiction-years came to be reckoned as beginning on September 1, and a Byzantine "Feast of the Indiction" was fixed on that day. In England, on the other hand, the system of dating, probably introduced by Bede himself, reckoned the indiction-years as beginning on September 24, and hence we know that for the document of Pope Gregory in chapter 23 the fourteenth indiction-year fell between 24 September 595 and 24 September 596.[4]

Book I.24

Etherius was really bishop of Lyons. The archbishop of Arles at this time was Vergilius. This letter was one of a batch of eight commendatory letters sent by Pope Gregory on behalf of St. Augustine and his companions to various bishops and secular rulers.

Book I.25

Here is the story of the conversion of Ethelbert (commonly so spelled, but "AEthelberht" in the Oxford text), King of Kent, who thus becomes the first Christian king in England. His wife, Bertha, was a member of the Frankish royal house. At the time of Augustine's arrival on the Isle of Thanet, Ethelbert had already been married for some thirty years. Supposing Bertha to be a faithful Christian, one can hardly imagine that

---

4. For further information on this fascinating but very complicated subject, one may consult the opening pages of C. R. Cheney, ed., *A Handbook of Dates for Students of British History* (Royal Historical Society Guides and Handbooks no. 4). New edition revised by Michael Jones (Cambridge and New York: Cambridge University Press, 2000).

Ethelbert had not already heard something of the rewards that Christianity had brought to Clovis and his Frankish successors, if not from his wife then perhaps from Liudhard, bishop of Senlis, who had been sent with her to England as her chaplain. Here, also, was a religion that would draw him and his kingdom nearer to the wealthy and civilized axis of Mediterranean life. Now that the Augustinian mission had come to England, he could convert to the Christian faith without the embarrassing implications of dependence upon the Franks. As his queen was Frankish, to go one step further in his alliance with the Franks by taking her religion might have been seen by his local political allies as obsequiousness toward the Franks had it not been for Augustine's mission. (Further on Ethelbert, see II.5, below.)

From sources external to Bede, we know that the earliest surviving document of an English king to use the phrase *Dei Gratia* ("by the Grace of God") in the royal title, apparently taken over from the style already in use by bishops, comes from Ethelbert and is dated to the year 605.

There are several items of cultural interest in this chapter, of which the first is the curious measurement of the "hide." The *hide* of land varied in size up to about 120 acres. It was a unit of agricultural potential rather than of geographic area, indicating the amount of land considered adequate for a family or household. Thus a rocky promontory of several square miles might only be one hide, whereas a fertile valley of the same size would have been measured as being of many more hides.

Later on, when Ethelbert receives Augustine and his delegation, Bede informs his readers both of the reception and of the reason behind it: "Sitting in the open air," Ethelbert "took care that they should not meet in any building." While Bede ascribes this act by King Ethelbert to pagan suspicion, it is also likely that the king normally held such audiences in the open air, and it is unlikely that there was any suitable hall near the riverside where they could meet.

The Christian customs of the day are displayed equally well in this passage. As the public procession approached the king, Bede notes that the monks were carrying both a silver cross and "the image of our Lord and Saviour painted on a panel" *(in tabula depictam)*. The description of the latter brings to mind an *eikon,* or icon, which would not be regarded as remarkable in that they were already used in both East and West at that time. It is noteworthy that Bede says they carried this "image" (his Latin word is *imago*) "in accordance with their custom," which seems to imply that such devotional objects were already familiar and known at Canterbury then.[5]

The missionary zeal for evangelism in the early saints of Britain and Ireland came primarily in the form of preaching, and we note that here, Augustine sits to preach and teach, as was the custom of teachers in the ancient world and of the early fathers. Standing to preach from a pulpit was first made popular by St. John Chrysostom in the later fourth century.

King Ethelbert's response to Augustine's preaching was quite tolerant: "We will receive you hospitably and provide what is necessary for your support; nor do we forbid you to win all you can to your faith and religion by your preaching." This royal policy of toleration is similar to, and seems to operate much like, Constantine's initial policy towards Christians after he had won the battle of the Milvian Bridge in 312. As with Constantine, the growth of Christianity in the realm also signals an increase in the piety of the king. From this beginning, Augustine and his companions went to Canterbury in procession, singing and carrying the cross and image of their Lord. The text that they sang, noted at the end of this chapter, is the Gallican Rogation Day antiphon for processions, from Daniel 9:16.

Book I.26

Augustine of Canterbury is Bede's first model bishop. Although we do not hear of them all immediately, others included Aidan, Chad, and Cuthbert, who are also held up by Bede as models for emulation. Bede's ideal apparently comes from St. Gregory the Great's *Book of Pastoral Care* and frequently appeals back to the "primitive church," although Bede was not the first (or the last) to make such an appeal. An earlier example can be found in the fifth-century spiritual writer named Cassian. In particular, Bede associates the "primitive church" with the concept of "apostolic poverty" and the holding of all goods in common. Bede recommends this as an ideal for his

5. See Christopher P. Kelley, "Canterbury's First Icon," *Sobornost* 7, no. 3 (Summer 1976): 193-97.

own time, even though such poverty was not understood to be "absolute" or "complete" in the sense that it became with the later religious orders of Franciscans and Dominicans (cf. Books I.27, IV.23, IV.27).

With regard to their place of worship Bede remarks that "There was nearby, on the east of the city, a church built in ancient times in honour of Saint Martin, while the Romans were still in Britain, in which the queen who, as has been said, was a Christian, used to pray." This church is today regarded as being the earliest place of Christian worship in England still in use. Most of the foundations of the present church are probably post-Roman in date, but it also incorporates some Roman and pre-Roman material, and some portions of the current structure, especially of the south chancel wall and the west wall, are indeed Roman and date to the fourth century. It does seem probable that the present eleventh-century baptismal font in the church also incorporates parts of an older font that was used in the church at the time of Bede. The choice of St. Martin of Tours as the patron of the church stems no doubt from the fact that he was the patron saint of Bertha's family in Paris. The reader should be aware, however, of the possibility that over the course of time this church of St. Martin may have become confused with the nearby church of Saint Pancras, now in ruins.

Certain liturgical phrases that come up in the Latin lose a portion of their significance in the translation into English. When Bede says that the group began "to say mass," his actual words are *"missas facere,"* meaning to "make" the Mass or "do" the Mass. The earliest use of this phrase, *missas facere,* is said to be from St. Ambrose, Bishop of Milan in the late fourth century (Epistle 20.4). Bede's reference "to baptize" here seems to imply font-baptism as also in Book III.7; however, baptism by immersion appears to be the practice referenced in II.14.

Bede in I.26 assumes that Ethelbert was one of the earliest converts, and it would seem logical that Augustine would have been the one to baptize him, but we know for certain only that he had been baptized by the time of his death, probably in 616. Whatever the circumstances and date, the king now tolerates and even favors Christianity in what is the remote beginnings of the royal endowment of the see of Canterbury. Inasmuch as paganism is still strong, however, the king will not compel persons to accept the Christian faith, having "learned from his teachers and guides in the way of salvation that the service of Christ was voluntary and ought not to be compulsory." All this notwithstanding, there is frequently a connection between evangelism and miracles in Bede, as here in I.26 we read that Ethelbert and his court proceeded to conversion and baptism once the truth of Augustine's witness had been confirmed by "many miracles." Often in Bede we find an evangelistic dimension of miracle and a miraculous dimension of evangelism that feed and reinforce each other.

Book I.27

The replies of Pope Gregory the Great to the questions of St. Augustine of Canterbury offer a wealth of insight into the life of the church in the sixth and seventh centuries. Although it has been argued that all these replies, or *Responsiones,* were forged around the year 731, this view has been largely discredited.[6] Note again that Vergilius, not Etherius, was archbishop of Arles (cf. I.24). There is no longer much reason to think that Augustine went back over to France, possibly Arles, for consecration as bishop at some point after he had been in England for a while, a matter on which Bede seems rather confused, and it seems more likely that Augustine was already consecrated in France, possibly at Autun, on his way to England between July 596 and September 597. Laurence, the priest whom Augustine is said to have sent to Rome with his letter, is the same Laurence who will become Augustine's successor as archbishop of Canterbury in 604 (cf. II.4). We now proceed to the nine questions and answers as Bede has recorded them.

The first question deals primarily with Augustine's role as bishop and the administrative tasks of his diocese. Pope Gregory's response about the

6. For some reviews of scholarly opinion about this series of questions and answers, see Margaret Deanesly, *The Pre-Conquest Church in England* (London: A. & C. Black, 1961), pp. 130-33; Henry Mayr-Harting, *The Coming of Christianity to England* (New York: Schocken Books, 1972), pp. 269-71; and Paul Meyvaert, "Bede's Text of the *Libellus responsionum* of Gregory the Great to Augustine of Canterbury," pp. 15-33 of *England Before the Conquest: Studies in Primary Sources Presented to Dorothy Whitelock* (Cambridge: Cambridge University Press, 1971). Many have written about these questions and the replies given to them.

duties of the bishop begins with reference to the Scripture of 1 Timothy 3:1-7, which is the classical and oft-repeated definition of a bishop's duties. The fourfold division of revenues noted here was widespread throughout the Middle Ages, and it allows Bede to return to one of his favorite themes mentioned in the previous chapter, the connection of the primitive church with the sharing of goods. Gregory's advice to clergy about marriage is worth noting. Pope Gregory does in fact counsel that "clerics but in minor orders" should be married if they "cannot be continent." The typical rule and practice in the medieval church is seen here, namely that "major" clerics (bishops, priests, and deacons) could not marry but "minor" clerics could. At this time and up to the early thirteenth century, the order of subdeacon was considered "minor," but in 1207 Pope Innocent III defined it as being "major."

Echoes of Scripture occur regularly throughout this discussion, strengthening the tie between monastic poverty and the early church. The principle that "division is to be made to each according to his need" comes from Acts 4:35, while the last sentence of this section beginning with the exhortation to "give alms" is from Luke 11:41.

We also note here that Gregory refers to "the English Church" (*ecclesia Anglorum,* literally "the church of the English") as having been lately converted to the faith. Such reference to the conversion of the people of an already existent church in England may well be testimony to the presence of an independent form of Christianity already there prior to Augustine's missionary efforts.

Augustine's second question about a standardized style of worship provides a platform for one of Gregory's most oft-quoted remarks: that Augustine should make a careful selection of the customs he finds and "teach the Church of the English, which is still new in the faith, what you have been able to gather from other churches. For things are not to be loved for the sake of a place, but places are to be loved for the sake of their good things." The list of possibilities is of interest, the Latin reading *sive in Romana sive in Galliarum seu in qualibet ecclesia,* that is "in the Roman or the Gaulish or any other church." Though not apparent in translation here, Bede quotes Gregory as using the adjectival form of "Roman" to describe the Roman Church but the genitive forms of "peoples" to describe the church in various lands or national territories ("Church of the English," "Church of the Gauls": *Anglorum, Galliarum*). Despite such a prevailing tolerance on the part of Gregory I, a policy of Romanization would later come to be urged by his successor Gregory VII in the late eleventh century. It should be noted, however, that such a policy of variegated tolerance was already well on the way to being adjusted and even reversed before then. This can be seen from the last part of the last sentence of this very paragraph, which takes for granted that a particular form of liturgy will be established ("collected into one bundle"), and from the fact that Augustine himself apparently did not follow Gregory's advice, as the Roman Mass soon began to prevail over much of England.

The third question, about punishing those who rob churches, offers some insight into the outlook of the church at the time about such matters. That the punishment should take into account the motivation for the offense, a concept that we see here, was not an element present in Anglo-Saxon law. Gregory takes special care to remind Augustine that the punishment must fit the crime and its cause, and that it must not be influenced by anger. Gregory advises him to remember that the church punishes like a parent rather than in strict retribution. Furthermore, the church is not to profit from the restoration of stolen goods. On the other hand, as we know from other sources, King Ethelbert, influenced by Germanic law, went much further than Pope Gregory advised, and decreed *twelve*-fold restoration of church property. Even the later moderation of the Penitential of Theodore of Tarsus, written under Irish influence, prescribed only fourfold restitution.

Questions number four and five suggest that Augustine has encountered a number of new customs, among them the prevalent Anglo-Saxon custom of marriage to one's stepmother. A notable instance soon to occur was the marriage of Ethelbert's son Eadbald to his father's widow, not Bertha but a second wife. Some scholars regard this text within Bede as not coming from Pope Gregory but rather a later addition intended to cater to Germanic conditions. Their reason for this skepticism is that in the western church the prohibition of marriage by degrees did not come as early as Bede. The Scripture quotations here are Leviticus 18:7 (the first two), Matthew 19:5, and John 14:6. The pastoral rationale upon which the fifth reply ends sounds very much like Gregory the Great: "For in these days the holy Church corrects some things with zeal and tolerates some things with gentleness, while in her wisdom she connives at other things and so by forbearance and connivance often succeeds in checking the evil which she resists."

The sixth question addresses the very practical concern for Augustine of being a missionary bishop stationed on the very edge of the Roman Empire: Can a bishop ordain another bishop by himself? With his characteristic common sense Gregory points out that there is at the beginning only one answer to the question: yes, where Augustine is as yet the only bishop. His response points to his desire to remain true to the earlier traditions that have been established in the church. Canon 4 of the first ecumenical council of Nicaea in 325 had stipulated no less than three bishops for consecration, and there were other similar precedents. These laws did not pronounce consecration by a single bishop invalid, however, in which case Gregory's advice would likely have been different, but rather seem to have been intended to prohibit clandestine consecrations. Later, when more bishops become available near at hand, Gregory says that the custom earlier established in the church of needing three or four bishops for consecration must prevail. The Latin phrase that begins Gregory's reply, *Anglorum ecclesia,* is variously rendered in different translations as "Church of the English," "English Church," and "Church in England," but only the first is technically correct.

The next question might be seen as a case of Augustine trying to claim jurisdiction over the older established diocese of Gaul, but in all likelihood this is not the case. It might be suggested that Augustine had in mind jurisdiction over the French clergy in Kent, but "all the bishops of Britain" is probably intended to indicate the Celtic bishops in the West. At the beginning of Gregory's answer to this question, we should note the reference to the *pallium* as a symbol of dignity conferred by Popes upon metropolitan archbishops as a sign of their jurisdictional authority (that is, over a major region). Like a circular white stole in appearance and marked with four or six crosses that were originally pinned but later embroidered upon it, the pallium looked like a double-Y when worn on the front and back and around the neck. It was woven of lamb's wool in the convent of St-Agnes-outside-the-Walls at Rome and placed first upon the tomb of St. Peter before conferral by the Pope or his representative. Continuing in use in the Roman Catholic Church today, it was discontinued in Anglican use at the English reformation but can still be seen in the arms of the see of Canterbury. (See also I.29.)

Questions eight and nine are generally regarded as being later, composed probably at Canterbury and based on moral theology lectures given there after Augustine's time. Such a judgment seems well founded given the difference in the immediacy of the questions and their lengthy and more theologically involved answers. Regarding the questions about the rights and responsibilities of mothers, expectant or recently delivered, the answers reveal both careful thought and gracious pragmatism and do not portray Gregory as being fundamentalistic in his interpretations of Scripture. Baptism is seen as a gift of grace and as such should never be withheld on legalistic grounds, especially in the face of the imminent or potential demise of the seeker. As for the old question of "the churching of women," the reply deals admirably with the texts of Scripture without dismissing them, even making reference to Leviticus 12:4-5 and preferring a thorough treatment based on the doctrine of original sin and an understanding of the difference between the covenants of Old and New Testaments rather than making a cursory dismissal. Whatever views may be held on such matters, Bede does record Gregory as clearly stating the classical catholic position: "Fleshly copulation is lawful when it is for the sake of producing offspring and not of desire; and the fleshly intercourse must be for the sake of producing children and not the satisfaction of vicious instincts."

The final question of this section, while prompted by the occurrence of unbidden thoughts of sexual fantasies or "illusions" in the form of dreams, offers insight into the prevailing theology of sin and sexuality at the time. This description of the three modes of temptation is borrowed from Pope Gregory's homily for the first Sunday of Lent. This three-step process Gregory had described as taking place by suggestion, by growth in pleasure, and by consent to completion. It is of note that Gregory has passed up an opportunity to appeal directly to Scripture, where James 1:14-15 puts forth a similar three-step process under the names of desire, sin, and death. The Latin text of Bede reflects the thought of St. Augustine of Hippo in its preoccupation with the body and asceticism. Some scholars regard the ninth question and answer as a later addition, possibly composed at Canterbury. The question itself, which in Latin ends with the phrase *sacra mysteria celebrare,* confirms the use of "holy mysteries" as a term for the Eucharist or Mass already at this time in England, and is to be compared with the term *missarum solemnia celebrare* ("to celebrate the solemn rites of the mass") that occurs shortly below.

Book I.28

As has been noted earlier at I.4, Vergilius was not successor to Etherius. This chapter seems to extend the discussion from question number seven in the previous chapter about the relationship between Augustine and the bishops of Gaul.

Book I.29

Here is the account of Pope Gregory's second mission to England (in 601). From the list of characters, a number come to occupy important positions in the church. Mellitus, Justus, and Paulinus became the bishops of London, Rochester, and York, respectively. Mellitus and Justus later became Augustine's second and third successors at Canterbury after Laurence. With these missionaries Pope Gregory has also seen fit to send "all such things as are generally necessary for the worship and ministry of the Church." Particularly intriguing among the items on his list of necessities are the "relics of the holy apostles and martyrs" and "very many manuscripts." One may assume the relics are to go within or upon or behind or alongside the altars of the new places of worship that will surely result from the missionary endeavor. Regarding the "many manuscripts," Professor Deanesly comments:

> Among the codices sent by Gregory to Augustine at the hands of abbot Mellitus one has survived, and has some bearing on the question of what rite Augustine used at Christ Church. It is a beautifully illuminated

altar book: but Gregory would have sent it for use, not merely the adornment of the chapel. Augustine must originally have brought a
sacramentary with him from Rome: perhaps the only book he brought
beside a Psalter: but he would, in general, have used the books sent him
later by the Pope, with such modifications or additions as he saw fit.

The surviving gospel book (Corpus Christi College, Cambridge,
MS. 286) is accepted by palaeographers as having been written in Italy in
the mid sixth century. It once belonged to St. Augustine's abbey, for documents concerning the abbey were written into the manuscript. It may
well have been among the altar books kept with the relics of the abbey,
not in the monastic library, for manuscripts thus preserved in the trea-
sury had a better chance of surviving pillage and even the abandonment
of the house: the holy relics would be the first things saved in an alarm,
and the gospel book with them. The manuscript thus survived the Danish raids, was at St. Augustine's in the eleventh century, and was given by
Matthew Parker [archbishop of Canterbury 1559-1575] to Corpus Christi
College, Cambridge.

In the manner of gospel books for altar use at the day, this fine vel-
lum manuscript had originally canon tables, a portrait of the evangelist at
the beginning of each gospel, of which only that of St. Luke has survived,
and a page divided rectangularly and illuminated with small scenes from
the gospel. The portrait of St. Luke also has gospel scenes painted into
the design: and if all the evangelists' pictures had similar scenes, the gospel book may have had as many as 70 little gospel pictures. One of great
liturgical interest is that of the Last Supper, entitled *Cena domini;* Christ
in the middle of a group of eight disciples is seated at a round table (those
facing him are omitted): the cup is before him and in the centre of the table the paschal lamb of the Passover: he holds the bread in his left hand
and blesses with his right, and the three disciples on his right hand copy
his gesture. The scene is in fact a representation of the Last Supper as a
concelebration, such as took place at Rome on solemn occasions in Augustine's day, and, indeed, ever since. It is a very old picture, very old
teaching: Christ himself celebrates what was, in Augustine's day, already
colloquially called 'the mass', and with him his apostles.

It is a reasonable surmise that the Roman missionaries, using this

Italian altar book, would have celebrated according to contemporary Roman custom on a low square altar.[7]

Also in this chapter, Bede again uses the Latin construction *Anglorum Ecclesia* for the church in Britain, which means literally the "Church of the English." Here again, as in question seven of I.27 above, we see reference to the pallium, a long white cloth shaped something like a stole, that is here in transition from being merely a mark of papal favor to becoming a symbol of authority. Gregory's original plan for two ecclesiastical provinces (London and York) was based upon the old Roman administrative division into Upper and Lower Britain, with York and London (not Canterbury) as the principal cities. But in the end Augustine consecrated only two suffragans (literally "helpers," or assistant bishops) for the south of England and was able to do nothing about the north or about moving to London, which was a pagan stronghold outside the protection of King Ethelbert of Kent. There was no fully established archbishopric of York, nor twelve southern suffragans, until the late eighth century, and Kent, in which Canterbury was located, dominated Essex at the time that Augustine arrived. Nonetheless, it has well been remarked that these plans for the limits of the two provinces did nothing but sow the seeds of confusion and strife, which bore fruit in due season!

Book I.30

This letter of Pope Gregory is now thought to be later, rather than earlier, than Gregory's letter in Book I.32.[8] The preferred date for this letter is now 18 July. Quite apart from the academic issue of dating the letter, the practice of "christening" the pagan sites of worship is described here in some detail. The idols are to be destroyed, but the structures that contained them are to be aspersed and furnished with altars made holy with the relics of the saints, and the pagan sacrifices to be replaced by appropriate ceremonies of Chris-

7. Deanesly, *The Pre-Conquest Church,* pp. 59-60.
8. Cf. *Journal of Ecclesiastical History,* July 1971, p. 254; *Studies in Church History,* 1970, pp. 29-38.

tian worship. Gregory's hope seems to be that by utilizing places to which people were already accustomed in this way, the missionaries might gain more converts through convenience and familiarity than by a rigid and thorough rejection of the local culture. Note the assumption that aspersion (sprinkling) with holy water is necessary. The mention of enclosing relics within altars (discussed further in Book V.20) confirms their inclusion in the list of necessities in Book I.29. The suggestion that "some solemnity ought to be given in exchange" for pagan cult festivals was a time-honored practice from the earliest days of the Christian religion.

Book I.31

Gregory's attitude toward miracles and the purpose of them as he saw it is spelled out in this chapter. Upon hearing that Augustine had performed miracles, Gregory regards it necessary not to congratulate him, but rather to caution him. He quotes from Luke chapter 10, "In this rejoice not, but rather rejoice that your names are written in heaven." Here we see that miracles are for Gregory both a good thing and something to be feared if their purpose is forgotten. Gregory's understanding of their purpose as recorded by Bede in this chapter is that by them "the souls of the English are drawn through outward miracles to inward grace." Gregory's word for miracle which Bede quotes is *miraculum*, "miracle," in contrast to Bede's preferred nomenclature for such events, which he calls by the Latin word *signum* or "sign," which has a somewhat different connotation. Here, as the thought of Gregory is expounded by Bede, they are given by God for the power of salvation. But miracles, no less than decisions of synods, the enthroning and dethroning of kings, the consecrations of bishops, the travels of missionaries, are all seen by Bede as indications of God's presence and action in history.

Book I.32

In this letter from Gregory to Ethelbert, there is an echo of the political terminology seen earlier in the discussion of the various churches. As the church in England was not the "Church of England" but rather "the Church of the English people," so also King Ethelbert is the "King of the English," *Rex Anglorum.* English kings did not style themselves as "King of England," *Rex Angliae,* on documents or seals until the beginning of the reign of King John (1199). Pope Gregory cites the Emperor Constantine as a model Christian ruler for King Ethelbert to emulate and warns him of the situation at hand: "The end of the world is at hand, as we learn from the words of Almighty God in the holy scriptures; and the kingdom of the saints which knows no end is near." This millenarian eschatology, based upon Revelation 20:2-7 and the view that the world's end was approaching in the year 1000, was a widespread Christian belief in Bede's day.

Book I.33

This chapter records the founding of Christ Church, Canterbury, under Augustine in 597, which is now Canterbury Cathedral and which can be visited at their interesting website, www.Canterbury-Cathedral.org. This is what became of the old Roman church that Augustine repaired after it was given him by King Ethelbert. The other church, east of the city, which Augustine founded and dedicated to "the blessed apostles Peter and Paul," became the home of a monastery that would become the burial place of most of the seventh-century archbishops and the Kentish kings. The monastery later became St. Augustine's where Albinus was to become abbot (see Bede's Preface). This was apparently the first Benedictine house to be established outside of Italy. The story of the miraculous appearance of light over a grave is the first of many post-mortem attestations of holiness that Bede records.

Book I.34

This chapter appears to be a further illustration of the ongoing political turmoil between the pagan north and the Christian south. The material here seems to serve mainly as a functional end to the political and physical geographical references that governed much of the contents of Book I.

Book II.1

Book II tells of Pope Gregory the Great, founder of the papal mission to England, who "made our nation, till then enslaved to idols, into a church of Christ." Since it was Gregory who dispatched Augustine to England to become the first archbishop of Canterbury, and in many ways Gregory is the real hero in Bede's account of the spread of Christianity in England, Gregory is "at least an apostle to us," Bede says. It is therefore appropriate to devote some attention at this point to this remarkable person, who has been rightly named the last of the patristic Popes of the early church and at the same time the first of the Popes of the Middle Ages. Bishop of Rome and therefore Pope from 590 to 604 (Bede's date of 605 is ahead by one year), Gregory on the worldwide scale was at this very point in his career poised to become the chief architect of the emerging Latin and Rome-centered church of the Western Middle Ages that has lasted well into our time. His political and administrative savvy established the church as the dominant force on the Italian peninsula. He was responsible for the major early development of the papal states, building upon temporal endowments of land that dated back to the emperor Constantine in the early fourth century, ensuring that every Pope after his reign on into the nineteenth century was also a petty Italian prince.

For centuries to follow, Gregory's missionary impulse (notably his sending of Augustine to England), his promotion of biblical studies and liturgical unity, his pastoral sensitivity, his exemplary episcopal manner, and his Benedictine spirituality in the context of monastic living, not to mention his many writings, his letters, his homilies on the Gospels, his *Dialogues,* and his commentaries on many books of the Bible, all left an indelible mark on the church throughout Europe and beyond. It has well been remarked that his pontificate and personality did much to establish the understanding both in thought and in reality that the papacy was the supreme authority in the church. "Servant of the servants of God" was the title he chose for himself and exemplified in his own life and also bequeathed to his successors. The book for which he is best known was also the first writing to come from his pen after he ascended the papal throne in 590; published about the year 591, his *Book of Pastoral Care*[9] still today remains the most widely read and single most influential book in the Christian pastoral tradition.[10] St. Augustine took a copy of it with him in 596 when Gregory sent him on mission to England, and Bede himself near the end of his life commended this treatise as a remedy for corruptions he perceived in the English Church. It is fair to say that "Gregory's Shepherd's Book," as it was sometimes called, set the tone for pastoral ministry in the English Church of Bede's time and for long thereafter.

Here in Bede's discussion of Gregory's commentary on Job, we see Gregory's approach to Scriptural interpretation, revealing the breadth of meanings that were of interest to biblical scholars of his age. Bede here indicates that Pope Gregory followed a threefold interpretation of Scripture: 1) the literal or historical meaning; 2) the allegorical or mystical meaning, "its bearing on the mysteries of Christ and the Church"; and 3) the tropological, or moral, meaning, "the sense in which it applies to each of the faithful." A great part of modern nineteenth- and twentieth-century historical-critical scholarship on the Bible has focused exclusively on the first of these three, the literal and historical meaning, to the exclusion of the other two aspects of Gregory's interest. The second, the allegorical or mystical meaning, has rarely been admitted in mainline liberal scholarship since the time of the eighteenth-century Enlightenment with its attendant distrust of authority and tradition. Finally, Gregory's interest in the potential moral application of Scripture has been largely relegated to the more conservative and fundamentalistic traditions. Unlike many modern interpreters of Scripture, however, Gregory and others of his day did not feel the need to privilege any one of these hermeneutical approaches to the detriment of the others. In the present, it would seem that the pendulum is swinging back to the broader approach that was held by Gregory and Bede in their own time.

Initially confusing even to students of church history is the reference

9. Entitled in the Penguin translation of Bede as *The Pastoral Office* and in the Oxford translation simply as *Pastoral Care*.

10. In English translation it is available both in the Nicene and Post-Nicene Fathers, second series volume 12, and also in the Ancient Christian Writers series volume 11, reprinted by Paulist Press.

here to one "Eutychius," patriarch of Constantinople who died in 582, whose heretical views about the impalpable nature of our resurrection bodies Gregory is said to have refuted earlier while he was papal representative to that city. This person is not, however, to be confused with Eutyches, the archimandrite at Constantinople whose "monophysite" heresy (that the Word after becoming flesh had only one nature) was condemned earlier at the fourth ecumenical council of Chalcedon in 451.

Also notable are Gregory's liturgical decrees regarding the celebration of Mass (*missae celebrarentur* is Bede's Latin term). Gregory ordered that Mass should be celebrated over the tombs of Peter and Paul, which could be done now that a reconstruction of Peter's tomb in his time apparently enabled Mass to be celebrated westward using the top of the shrine as an altar. A number of clauses cited here from the *Hanc igitur* section of the Roman canon of the Mass thus are thought to derive from the forms introduced by Gregory himself. Regarding Gregory's own death, some older printings of the Penguin text read "His body was laid to rest on March the fourth," but this was an error and it has been corrected in more recent editions and other translations to "March 12," the Latin reading *"die quarto iduum Martium."* This date came to be reflected in modern church observances of the feast of St. Gregory, although more recently the new calendar of the Roman Catholic Church now assigns his feast to September 3, the date of his ordination, because March 12 frequently falls in Lent. In the Anglican Communion, the Roman Church's date of September 3 is now followed in the Church of England, whereas the date of March 12 is still observed in the calendar of the Episcopal Church in the U.S.A.

Of further interest here is the Latin phrase used by Bede to describe the place where Pope Gregory's body was buried. Although earlier Penguin editions translated *Ante secretarium* in the paragraph that precedes the epitaph of Gregory as "before the sacristy," it is now correctly rendered in the current Penguin, as also in the Oxford translation, as "before the sanctuary." Its subsequent history is revealing, for King Alfred's late-ninth-century Anglo-Saxon translation of Bede rendered *secretarium* as *husulportice. Husul* was the Anglo-Saxon word for "sacrifice" or "oblation" and hence for "Eucharist," whereas the literally proper Anglo-Saxon word for *secretarium* (English "sanctuary") would have been simply *portice.* A side chapel or chamber adjacent to a church was thus called a *portice,* but the fact that *secretarium* was by the late ninth century not being rendered simply *portice* but rather *husulportice* suggests very strongly that by King Alfred's time the Eucharist itself was normally being kept (reserved) in a side chapel or adjacent chamber (that might be called a *secretarium,* sacristy, *portice,* or, most commonly, *husulportice*).

The hymn-like epitaph of Pope Gregory was later incorporated, with alteration, into the sixth and ninth lessons of the Sarum Breviary Office for the Feast of the Translation of St. Thomas Becket's Relics, July 7: "Let the nation of the Angles rejoice in the Lord, which the heavenly King distinguished in a special manner before others, when he preferred from it a man without blemish, that thus one of the Angles might be established among the Angels."

The related story of Gregory's discovery of the English slave-boys has been questioned by some as being too tidy to be true, and Gregory's puns may indeed prove trying for critical readers to digest. He mishears the Latin noun *angli* (Angles, the tribe) as *angeli* (angels), also the Latin *Deira* which was the kingdom of origin of these particular slaves was again misheard as *de ira* (the wrath of God), and finally the reference to Aelle as their king becomes "alleluia" to Gregory's spiritual hearing. Despite a cleverness that seems almost remarkable, the authenticity of this story about Gregory and the fair-haired English slave-boys, an incident that probably occurred in the Roman marketplace around 585-588, is upheld in the works of many leading scholars.

Book II.2

This chapter describes an early attempt by Augustine to persuade the Celtic Christians to adopt Roman practice. These Christians were scattered throughout England and Ireland to the north and west of the primary Roman missionary influence. The reader may at first be confused by Bede's nomenclature, and references to "the bishops and teachers in the neighboring British kingdom" who "did not keep Easter at the proper time" should be understood as referring to the Celtic Christians located to the west. Bede does not think highly of these people, and describes them as "preferring their own traditions to those in which all the churches throughout the world agree in Christ." The site of Augustine's Oak is uncertain; a possible location is Aust, on the Severn River. The controversy about the date of Easter resurfaces throughout Bede's *History;* further, see Appendix Four below. The use of miracles as a test between rival religious factions was a time-honored means of establishing the superiority of true Christianity in a pre-Enlightenment world that expected proof of this sort. Here Bede recounts a miracle, the restoration of sight to the blind, as evidence of Roman superiority over Celtic. "At once the blind man's sight was restored," Bede comments, "and all acknowledged Augustine to be a true herald of the heavenly light."

The beginning of the second conference between Augustine's party and the British (Celtic) bishops turns on the advice of "a certain holy and prudent man who lived as a hermit" from the Celtic side who counsels that his bishops should consider abandoning their own traditions but only if Augustine is a "man of God," and that they can ascertain that by observing whether he rises to greet them. As it happened, Bede reports, Augustine remained seated and did not rise, and this angered the other group. Bede presents the British (Celtic) bishops as rather stubborn and Augustine's attitude as a mixture of dislike, indifference, and inflexibility towards them. Perhaps Augustine was following the custom whereby Roman magistrates were known not to rise at the entrance of those who sought their judgment, and Augustine may have decided to follow this tradition. (The practice is not unknown in some strata of society in some parts of the world even today, especially in ecclesiastical and courtly circles.)

Augustine remains firm and immediately presents three demands: observance of the Roman dating of Easter ("at the proper time"), use of the Roman baptismal rites and customs, and preaching to be done in fellowship with the Roman missionaries, all of which assert the primacy of Roman custom over Celtic. The dating of Easter was the most prominent of the three as it was the point of origin for the whole liturgical calendar, the moment of resurrection when heaven breaks into earth and time crosses with eternity, thus directly linked to the observance of the central feast of the Christian year. The practice of baptism in the Celtic churches was variable and is not known for certain, but it may have been reserved to adults only, possibly done without chrismation (anointing with holy oil), and possibly administered by means of only a single immersion (not threefold).[11] Also it may have been accompanied by a washing of feet. Whatever the differences over baptism may have been, it must have made sense, at least to Augustine and the Roman side, that there should be a norm to be followed by all the missionaries in a given area.

Bede reports that Augustine is said to have warned the other side that if they refused compliance they might suffer death at the hands of their enemies (the English), an example of the prevailing theology of retribution whereby it was thought that God punishes those who are not on God's side. Such a doctrine had roots deep in the Old Testament, especially in the books of 1 and 2 Chronicles, and is also part of Bede's overarching theme of England as being a promised land, with the implication that God does favor the Romans over the Celts. Bede reports that this warning, as predicted, was soon confirmed in the murder of the monks of Bangor by the forces of the pagan King Ethelfrid (spelled "AEthelfrith" in the Oxford text) at the battle of Chester *(Carlegion),* thus fulfilling Augustine's prophecy that "those heretics would also suffer the vengeance of temporal death because they had despised the offer of everlasting salvation." We note that Ethelfrid regards the Celtic monks who were praying against his forces as being enemies no less than those who were prepared to fight with swords.

Book II.3

Bede now shifts his focus back to Augustine as "archbishop of Britain" and to the consecrations of Mellitus and Justus as bishops, who had been sent as part of Pope Gregory's second mission in 601 (cf. I.29). The fact that Augustine consecrates Mellitus for London indicates that he chose not to obey Gregory's instructions to transfer himself there (I.29), although Bede does not take note of this decision on Augustine's part. Provision is made for

---

11. See Peter Cramer, *Baptism and Change in the Early Middle Ages, c.200-c.1150* (Cambridge: Cambridge University Press, 2002); Caitlin Corning, *The Celtic and Roman Traditions: Conflict and Consensus in the Early Medieval Church* (New York: Palgrave Macmillan, 2006), pp. 73-76.

weekly requiem Masses every Saturday in memory of Pope Gregory and Archbishop Augustine, who may have died in the same year of 604. The exact year of Augustine's death is uncertain, however, and it could have been any time from 604 to 609. Noteworthy in Augustine's epitaph, transcribed here by Bede, are the themes of mission, miracles, and worship of the true God. Feast days were established for both Gregory and Augustine as early as 747 at the Synod of Clovesho (Clofaeshoh). In the present time, St. Augustine of Canterbury is now kept in Anglican calendars both in England and America on May 26, and in the Roman Catholic Church on May 27 (the 26th being reserved for St. Philip Neri). St. Mellitus is generally commemorated on April 24, and St. Justus on November 10.

Book II.4

Augustine had named and consecrated his own successor, Laurence (cf. I.27), as archbishop. To do this was apparently against the canon law of the time; however, Bede sees no problem with his action. The reference to the early practice of St. Peter in the consecration of Clement as the second bishop of Rome may be taken as subtle critique of the current practice of Bede's own day, for Bede, like many after him, may have been looking back to the apostolic era as the pure and ideal period in the church's early history. The Scots and Britons are regarded as "unorthodox" by Bede, for they kept the Celtic date of Easter. The invitation of Pope Boniface IV (608-615) to Bishop Mellitus may indicate a growing concern for conformity in the Roman Church itself. The ancient Roman temple known as the Pantheon, which Pope Boniface procured and purified and consecrated for Christian worship, still stands today.

Book II.5

St. Ethelbert, King of Kent, is remembered as the first English Christian king, his traditional feast day of February 24 or 25 marking the day of his death. Through the influence of his Christian wife Bertha, it was he who had welcomed St. Augustine and the Roman mission in the year 597 (cf.

I.25). He is said by Bede to be buried in St. Martin's "chapel," the Latin text reading *porticus* and indicating something more like a side-chapel or even "porch," because the Roman civil law, introduced by Ethelbert himself, forbade burials technically "inside" a building (further see I.33, II.1).[12]

The deaths of Ethelbert and Sabert (spelled "Saeberht" in the Oxford text, an early-seventh-century king of the East Saxons under whom they accepted the Christian faith) obviously open the way to strong pagan reactions, and these in turn, as Bede tells us, soon prompt divine retribution. Mellitus is one of the monks who had been sent to England by Pope Gregory I in 601, and in 604 he had been consecrated a bishop by St. Augustine of Canterbury with London as his episcopal headquarters. When Sabert's three sons, who have reverted to idolatry, see Mellitus, who has become the first bishop of London, "celebrating solemn mass" in a church (presumably the church of St. Paul, which Ethelbert had built for his use) and giving the Eucharist to the people, they ask the bishop why he will not give them the same "white bread" that he used to give to their father (whose nickname was "Saba"). Bishop Mellitus replies that if they are willing to be baptized, as was their father, then they may receive that Holy Bread as he did, but so long as they despise the life-giving waters (Latin: *lavacrum vitae,* literally "Water of Life") then they will certainly not receive the Bread of Life (Latin: *panem vitae*). To this decision about the necessity of baptism, they reply "We will not enter the font because we know that we have no need of it," although, all the same, they "wish to be refreshed by the bread." Bede's Latin term for "refreshed" is *refici volumus,* but he gives no further clue as to what they really wanted or why they wanted it. Bishop Mellitus again explains to the three royal brothers that no one can be admitted to communion without first being baptized, and they reply that if he refuses so trifling a request then they will have him and his followers banished from the kingdom, and this is what happens.

Mellitus retreats to Kent for consultation with his fellow bishop Justus of Rochester and, deciding to make no further issue of the matter at this time, together they flee across the Channel to Gaul. Nonetheless, retribution occurs, as Bede dutifully informs us, and the sons of Sabert and their army soon fall in

---

12. The word *porticus* is difficult to define. See "Porch and Porticus in Saxon Churches," *Journal of the British Archaeological Association,* Third Series, xx (London, 1956).

battle against the West Saxons. Eadbald, King of Kent, who has become a Christian and accepted baptism, soon recalls the bishops to England (616 AD), and Mellitus eventually becomes the third archbishop of Canterbury (619-624). He has clearly upheld the traditional, catholic, orthodox teaching on baptism, and even suffered for it. Some today, we should note, believe that the traditional teaching has been superseded by modern considerations and is not worth defending. But if it was only a trifling matter anyway, as the sons of Sabert exclaimed, then why not make peace with the rulers of the present age?

As a modern postscript, it is just possible that the sumptuous underground burial chamber of King Sabert, "defiantly buried by his sons in pagan splendor" (616 AD), has recently been discovered by archaeologists at Prittlewell near Southend in Essex. We shall probably never know for certain, but the recently published accounts of its discovery are intriguing.[13]

A comment must also be made about the sort of font that might have been used for baptism in very early England. If we may judge from the shapes of the six portable baptismal tanks that survive from this early period in England, the typical baptismal font in use at that time was probably a portable metal tank, possibly of lead, possibly decorated with a *Chi Rho* (the Greek initials that stand for Christ) and an *Alpha* and *Omega* (the first and last letters of the Greek alphabet, indicating that Christ is the beginning and the ending), or possibly the letters "VVA," indicating that Jesus Christ is the living water *(viva aqua)* as stated in John 4:10, the tank itself having low sides so that one could step into it.

Book II.6

The point of Bishop Laurence's dream, for Bede, seems to be that the concern and responsibility of Saint Peter, prince of the apostles, is asserted and demonstrably attested in it as the dream of the one who will be Canterbury's next archbishop. The result of Laurence's miraculous dream is more than a fresh determination, though, for he bears the marks of St. Peter's lash. The scars prove to be instrumental in the repentance of King Eadbald,

13. Ian Blair, "The Anglo-Saxon Prince," in *Archaeology* (September/October 2005): 25-29.

who is then baptized forthwith. So, by the intervention of none other than St. Peter himself, the church continues to be present in England. Next, Mellitus apparently succeeds Laurence as archbishop of Canterbury after he is unable to return to his see in London. During Mellitus's tenure as the archbishop, he builds a church "to the holy Mother of God" at Canterbury, of which the base of the west wall still stands.

Book II.7

The interplay of divine intervention with natural phenomena in the ongoing salvation-history of England is again seen in this chapter, as the prayers of Mellitus are instrumental in putting out the fire that was raging in Canterbury. This same story, in almost every detail, is also told of Marcellinus Bishop of Ancona earlier in the *Dialogues* of Gregory the Great (I.6) and was known to Bede, and (presumably) even to Mellitus as well. The ability to control the elements is a frequent feature in many of the miracles attributed to Celtic and early Roman saints in England and Ireland, although in this case Bede may be attempting to indicate that a natural explanation and a spiritual explanation are both involved in the same phenomenon. As with the stripes that Archbishop Laurence had received from St. Peter, so Mellitus's bodily infirmities seem to enhance rather than detract from his spiritual influence. The church of the Four Crowned Martyrs at Canterbury may have been founded under influence of the earlier dedication of a church of the same name on the Caelian Hill in Rome, which was located near the monastery of St. Andrew and would have been familiar both to Augustine and Gregory. The identification of the Four Crowned Martyrs is uncertain, although it is thought that they may have been four Persian Christian stonemasons who were martyred in the fourth century.

Book II.8

Justus follows Mellitus as archbishop of Canterbury. The conferral of the pallium upon Justus, mentioned near the end of the letter from Pope

Boniface V, now symbolizes his assumption of metropolitan authority under the Pope of Rome (cf. I.29). Note the use of the "majestic plural," which
we saw earlier in the letters of Pope Gregory. Justus is given the authority
"as occasion may require" (on his own) to consecrate bishops by Pope
Boniface. Pope Gregory had granted a similar permission to Augustine, but
Augustine had failed to multiply the number of bishops according to Gregory's original plan. Consequently, with the death of Mellitus there was
again no other bishop in reasonable geographic proximity who was in communion with the see of Canterbury in Britain at that time. There were, of
course, Celtic bishops in the kingdom, but these bishops were still observing Celtic rites and were, therefore, not in communion with Canterbury,
which observed Roman rites at that time.

Book II.9

This chapter introduces Bede's account of the conversion of Edwin, King of
Northumbria, the most important of the seven Anglo-Saxon kingdoms
(known as the "heptarchy") in the seventh century. The conversion of a
king in England at this time was of particular significance since it generally
entailed the conversion of his people. With this in mind, Bede's account begins with what appears to be a moralizing view of divine intervention in history, sometimes called a "Deuteronomic" view, in which God is seen as acting in history, as in the biblical book of Deuteronomy, to reward those who
have been faithful to God's wishes and to punish those who have been dis-
obedient. Edwin, who is yet a pagan, comes to a position of considerable
strength and brings more territory under control than any previous ruler in
England, as a sign of God's impending favor that will be granted him upon
his conversion to the Christian faith (which is still a long time to come, as
we learn from further reading).

Like Ethelbert, Edwin's conversion comes through the influence of his
wife. Edwin gives assurance that he is ready to accept the Christian religion
in return for the hand of Ethelberga (spelled "AEthelburh" in the Oxford
text), the daughter of Ethelbert, and in this way we are reminded of the similar story of the marriage of Bertha and Ethelbert (I.25). The stories of these

two royal conversions are almost carbon copies up to a point. Somewhat analogous to the role of Liudhard with Bertha, Paulinus (who had been sent to England with Mellitus and Justus by Pope Gregory in 601; cf. I.29) is now consecrated as bishop to accompany Ethelberga as her chaplain, and Bede tells us that Paulinus provides "daily instruction and the celebration of the heavenly sacraments" for her and her companions (literally, "daily celebration of the heavenly sacraments" *(cotidiana sacramentorum caelestium celebratione)*. Bede also tells us that Paulinus was consecrated bishop by Archbishop Justus of Canterbury on 21 July 625.[14] St. Paulinus is remembered in history as the first bishop/archbishop of York (and subsequently as bishop of Rochester), and his feast day is generally kept on October 10. Unlike the story of Ethelbert, however, Edwin gives his daughter Eanflaed in baptism (on the feast of Pentecost, a traditional day for it) as an advance pledge for God's promise to give him victory over his would-be assassin Cwichelm, King of the West Saxons. Victory is given to Edwin, yet Bede leaves his readers at the end of chapter 9 with Edwin unbaptized but still considering it and receiving a course of instruction from Bishop Paulinus.

Book II.10

Pope Boniface's letter to Edwin urging his conversion is a study unto itself. The conclusion of the letter first calls on Edwin to accept the sign of the Holy Cross and only after this to accept the other signs of a true conversion, namely baptism by water and the Holy Spirit. This belief in the power of the cross, for the Christians about whom Bede writes, goes beyond the merely symbolic and was quite widespread, perhaps through the influence of St. Athanasius' *Life of Antony,* which was well known from the fourth century onward. Carrying the cross as a standard and signing oneself with the cross were considered to be a method of protection from evil of all sorts.

---

14. For the opinion that the year 618 or 619 is more likely than 625, see D. P. Kirby, "Bede and Northumbrian Chronology," in *English Historical Review* 78 (1963): 514-27. See also S. Wood, "Bede's Northumbrian Dates Again," in *English Historical Review* 98 (1983): 280-96.

Book II.11

Another letter from Pope Boniface, this one to Ethelberga, also takes as its goal the conversion of Edwin to the Christian faith. The familiarity of Pope Boniface with the queen and her situation is remarkable and reveals the closeness of the ties between church and state, so to speak, at this time. Pressure is brought upon the queen, and gifts are given.

Book II.12

This chapter is difficult to place in its proper chronology. It seems at first to come before the time of Edwin and Ethelberga's marriage, but Bede places it after the letters from Pope Boniface V. In the end, the best explanation may be that it is a folktale, originating in Northumbria.[15] The exhortation of Paulinus at the end of the chapter tends to suggest that the gift of earthly rewards, in a more-or-less Deuteronomic way, is an indication of heavenly ones as well.

Book II.13

Bede in this chapter conflates three accounts of the conversion of King Edwin of Northumbria. The setting is a meeting of the "witan," or council of the king's wise men (laity as well as bishops), which was held at Yeavering (Northumberland). Portions of the great hall of the royal palace there, recently excavated, tend to confirm the physical arrangement that Bede suggests. Edwin asks his counselors what they think of this new religion, and Coifi the chief of the (pagan) priests (Latin, *primus pontificum*) and other senior counselors (Anglo-Saxon, "ealdormen") advance reasons largely of a pragmatic sort: "If, on examination, these new doctrines which have now

---

15. There is a much fuller explanation concerning this and other theories about the origin of this story in J. M. Wallace-Hadrill, *Bede's Ecclesiastical History: A Historical Commentary*, Oxford Medieval Texts (Oxford: Clarendon Press, 1988), pp. 70-71.

been explained to us are found to be better and more effectual, . . ." "If this new doctrine brings us more certain information, . . ." Such an attention to the practical benefits of religion was not limited to pagans, and can also be found in Celtic and other early Christian sources. The famous comparison of the span of human life with the flight of a sparrow through the warm banquet hall in the cold of winter, however, indicates a certain shift of reasoning from a purely physical reckoning of benefits to a more philosophical or even theological basis: "This is how the present life of man on earth appears in comparison with that time which is unknown to us. . . ." "So this life of man appears but for a moment; what follows or indeed what went before, we know not at all. . . ." The argument for acceptance of Christian teaching on the basis that it can reveal more certain knowledge, however, could easily leave the way open for still further, open-ended revelation at a later time, a possibility that is not raised in Bede's narrative.

Bede's careful use of terminology can be seen throughout this chapter and especially in his choice of words for "altar." In the phrase, "the temples and the altars which we have held sacred," there is an interesting exception to Bede's regular usage regarding altars and shrines. The "high priest of their religion" Coifi, who presumably doesn't know any better, is represented here as using the Latin word for a Christian altar, *altaria* (plural), rather than the pagan word *ara* which is what Bede's general principle would have called for (cf. I.7 above). After Coifi has begun to see the error of his ways, however, his terminology changes, and he himself becomes the first to lead the desecration and burning of the old pagan temples and altars (the Latin now correctly reflecting Bede's preferred term, *ara,* for a pagan altar or shrine). The location is at Goodmanham, near York, and Bede tells us that the crowd thought that Coifi was mad.

Coifi's action to terminate the local pagan cult cannot be passed over without some brief comment. The act of profaning the temple by casting a spear into it derives its symbolic meaning from the pagan religious tradition of the god Woden. Woden was said to have flung a spear over his enemies to defeat them; hence, Coifi on account of his recent change of heart appropriates one custom of the pagan culture in order to abolish another. There seems to be a contradiction, however, between Coifi's utter destruction of the shrine and the selection principle that had been proposed by Gregory the Great in his reply to St. Augustine's second question set forth above in I.27. Coifi's utter destruction of the shrine, apparently encouraged by Paulinus, seems to signal a complete break with paganism whereas Pope Gregory had been eager to allow at least some continuity and to build upon pagan habits or edifices whenever they might be put to Christian use. The conclusion of this section, that Coifi now "profaned and destroyed the altars which he himself had consecrated," is entirely to the point.

Book II.14

This chapter climaxes the story of the conversion and baptism of Edwin, King of Northumbria, and most of his royal house, at York in the year 627, "about 180 years after the coming of the English to Britain," Bede tells us. This event at the hand of Bishop Paulinus, in a simple wooden church on the site of the old Roman fort at York, the same site upon which Constantine had been proclaimed Caesar on the death of his father back in the year 306, is generally associated with the beginning of what would eventually become the great York Minster. (It can be visited today, either in person or by means of its extensive and inviting website at www.Yorkminster.org.) Bede himself once visited York, near the end of his life probably in 733, to consult with his former pupil Egbert about the state of the English Church at that time.

In recording the progress of Paulinus's preaching here, Bede hints at something that looks like a doctrine of predestination. The exact word in the Latin text is *praeordinati*, and it can be accurately translated "predestined" or "preordained." The Penguin edition opts for the former, stating that "as many as were predestined to eternal life believed and were baptized," whereas the Oxford translation prefers the word "foreordained." Such a doctrine, if Bede held it rigidly and consistently, would put his understanding of divine retribution, which assumes the free will to make a choice even against God (cf. II.2, above), at odds with Bede's sense of God's intention for England's national destiny ("the people whom He foreknew," as the Oxford text of I.22 puts it, or "the people whom he had chosen" in the Penguin translation).

Bede's subsequent account of the baptism of the two sons of Edwin provides a window into the practice of seventh-century baptismal rites in

England. Older Penguin translations said only that certain of Edwin's children died "soon after their baptism," whereas the Penguin edition now reads "while still wearing their white baptismal robes," which is more literal. The Oxford translation is even more literal, reading "while still wearing the chrisom," the latter word being a term that refers to the white garment customarily worn for a full week after baptism and named after the holy oil that was administered in Christian initiation and which this garment was intended to cover and bind. A term of ambivalent meaning even then, the "chrisom" at that time may have been merely the white cloth that was used to bind the oil of chrism on the forehead following the chrismation, or it may have been a full-sized robe that took its name from the same source. If death came within the octave of baptism (eight days afterward), such persons were therefore buried in their "chrisoms."

At the end of this chapter Bede provides an instance of baptism by immersion, and again at II.16. For baptisms performed in a font see I.26, II.5, and III.7. A preference for font-baptism does seem implied in Bede's closing explanation here that "they were not yet able to build chapels or baptisteries there in the earliest days of the church."

Book II.15

This chapter recounting the on-and-off attitude toward Christianity in East Anglia at that time is quite difficult to follow because of its frequent jumps in chronology. Raedwald, King of the East Angles and now ruler of all the provinces south of the Humber, apostatizes from his recently professed Christian faith and now takes out double insurance by means of two altars: "in the same temple he had one altar (*altare,* Christian) for the Christian sacrifice and another small altar (*arula,* diminutive of *ara,* the pagan word for altar) on which to offer victims to devils." Bede comments: "So his last state was worse than his first. After the manner of the ancient Samaritans, he seemed to be serving both Christ and the gods whom he had previously served." Scholars are divided as to whether Raedwald was the king who was laid to rest in the famous Sutton Hoo ship-burial near Woodbridge, Suffolk, the endnotes of the Penguin edition of Bede affirming it and the endnotes of the Oxford edition denying it. Raedwald's son, King Eorpwald, was converted by Edwin to the true Christian faith from Raedwald's syncretistic religion. Shortly after Eorpwald's conversion, however, he was killed by a pagan named Ricberht.

Book II.16

The close relationship of a deacon as assistant to the bishop which we see here was a role that went back as early as the beginnings of the third century, where it is found already in the document known as the *Apostolic Tradition* of Hippolytus. A striking detail in this chapter is the prominent role of just this sort of diaconal ministry. James the Deacon is noteworthy as the assistant to Bishop Paulinus at York, and he is presented here and in II.20 as the bishop's constant companion, acting in close cooperation with the bishop rather than serving in a local parish ministry or as an apprentice priest.

Also of interest in this chapter is the deference for the king's edict regarding the water stations along the highways (they were posts with brass bowls). In a peaceful Christian kingdom, at least in theory, as under King Edwin, the king rules out of the personal respect the subjects accord to the king, and not merely from force of law.

Book II.17

This chapter is almost entirely taken up by a letter of Pope Honorius I (625-38) to King Edwin. Edwin has apparently made some requests to the Pope regarding the future ordinations of bishops to replace Honorius at Canterbury (archbishop 627-53) and Paulinus at York, who would in due time receive their heavenly rewards. Hoping to avoid problems in the apostolic succession, Pope Honorius grants Edwin's request. The Pope's letter at one point refers to "*your* bishops," hinting at the close connection between church and state in Anglo-Saxon times; see comments on the "witan," or king's council, at II.13.

Book II.18

Pope Honorius makes provision that on the death of either of the archbishops of Canterbury or York the survivor is to have authority to appoint and consecrate a successor. (Augustine, we recall from II.4, had named and consecrated his own successor, Archbishop Laurence.) And as proof of this authority, he sends each of them a pallium, "so that you may carry out the consecration as God wills, by our authority and command." This is said to be granted on account of the long distance by sea and land. Although eventually in the Middle Ages the Popes alone will claim this right of appointment, the same reasoning of distance will continue in the grants of papal permission for legal cases to be tried in England rather than having to go to the court of Rome, which permissions in time came to be known as "the privilege of England."[16]

Book II.19

Pope John's coupling of the controversy over the date of Easter to the Pelagian heresy appears to be a clever piece of rhetoric attempting to heap disapproval upon two separate issues by linking them together and implying that a Pelagian might more likely be susceptible to acceptance of the wrong date for Easter. The two issues are in fact different, and a number of otherwise orthodox clergy did not observe the Roman date of Easter. For the Easter controversy see Book III and Appendix Four, below, and for Pelagianism, see above at I.9-10. Pope John's letter to the Irish churchmen has been dated to the year 640.

Book II.20

The death of King Edwin of Northumbria at the battle of Hatfield on 12 October 633, stands at the beginning of renewed tribal hostilities between

---

16. Cf. J. Robert Wright, *The Church and the English Crown, 1305-1334: A Study Based on the Register of Archbishop Walter Reynolds* (Toronto: Pontifical Institute of Mediaeval Studies, 1980), pp. 142-54.

the Celtic and Anglo-Saxon factions in England. Cadwalla was, according to Bede, a barbarian and false Christian, who paid no respect to the faith and religion of his political enemies, and Penda of Mercia, even worse, was an idolator. Throughout this chapter, Cadwalla and other "Britons" are Christians of the Celtic variety, whereas the "English" are depicted by Bede as holding the true faith, that is, they are Roman Christians. In the fallout of this strife, Paulinus flees with Queen Ethelberga to Kent, leaving behind his deacon James to care for the church of York. This was a big task, as the see of York was now left vacant for well over thirty years after the resignation of its first bishop, Paulinus, from 633 until Wilfrid in 664. Here, the same deacon mentioned in II.16 gets a somewhat fuller treatment. We note that his duties include baptisms and teaching, but Bede does not mention the Eucharist. In keeping with doctrine and tradition, deacons did not preside at celebrations of the Eucharist.

James the Deacon was also something of a choirmaster, and he taught his flock to "sing the music of the Church after the uses of Rome and Canterbury," as the Penguin translation puts it. This may be evidence of the continuing influence of Pope Gregory the Great, who did not originate the so-called Gregorian chant but had been instrumental in its popular acceptance. The Latin text of the foregoing quotation reads *iuxta morem Romanorum sive Cantuariorum,* which the Oxford translation renders "after the manner of Rome and the Kentish people," but it is difficult to infer, from this reference and the other slight evidence available, what system of church music was being taught by James the Deacon. It has been estimated that James lived somewhat past the age of ninety, "old and full of days" as Bede says. Other musical references in Bede are found in Book IV.2, 12, and 18, and in Book V.20.

Book III.1

Book III narrates the spread of Celtic Christianity in Northumbria and elsewhere and its confrontation with Roman Christianity in 664 at the Synod of Whitby, on the coast of north Yorkshire. Here the stormy fallout of Edwin's death is portrayed in much greater detail than in the final chapter of Book II. In recording the spread of Celtic Christianity in Northumbria, on the one hand Bede cannot be opposed to such saintly figures as Columba and Aidan, Celtic though they be, but on the other hand, Bede is quite certain that Roman Christianity is the true expression of the Christian faith. Throughout Bede's *History* this clash between Celtic and Roman factions is being played out, coming to a head at the Synod of Whitby. Book III.1 begins with a restatement of the familiar retribution dogma (that evil deeds are punished and good deeds are rewarded), as well as with an odd observation about historical revisionism. After recounting all the evils of Cadwalla and the apostasy of the sons of Ethelfrid ("AEthelfrith" in the Oxford translation), as well as Cadwalla's death and the accession of King Oswald, Bede notes that the events dating to the reigns of the apostate kings have been assigned to another king: "All those who compute the dates of kings have decided to abolish the memory of those perfidious kings and to assign this year to their successor Oswald, a man beloved of God." This is certainly an odd way of dealing with unpleasant historical evidence, but Bede, the consummate historian, has chosen to record all the information, letting his readers decide how they will handle the dating.

Bede could not control the way his work has subsequently been translated into English, however, and beginning at I.1 and noted again here and seen elsewhere the Latin words now translated in the Penguin and Oxford editions as "Irish" were usually in older Penguin editions translated as "Scots" or "Scottish." This may be confusing to anyone comparing an older Penguin edition with a modern one, since the Latin is the same and the earlier Penguin wording is actually a more literal rendering of the Latin. Presumably the later Penguin redactors decided that the earlier translations were misleading, which may be the reason why "Irish," instead of "Scottish," has now become the preferred Penguin translation of *Scotti, Scottos,* and *Scottorum* in most instances. The Oxford translation has opted for "Irish" since its first publication in 1969, as explained in the cautionary note near the end of the Introduction above.

Book III.2

The close relations of church and state that prevailed in most of the West for the medieval period are clearly evident in this chapter, as seen in King Oswald's piety. As with Augustine and his companions in Book I.25, Oswald understands the cross as more than a religious adornment. He sets up a cross in his camp as a standard to which he and all his men outwardly demonstrate their allegiance, even dipping splinters from its wood into drinking water for good health, a not uncommon practice in medieval Celtic and English spirituality.

The posture of kneeling for prayer, also seen here, was not the most common practice of the early church. More common in the second and third and fourth centuries was the *orans* position for prayer, that is, standing with hands outstretched to the heavens, but overall the custom has changed to kneeling by the time of King Oswald in the seventh century. To "sing the psalms" and to "offer up the holy sacrifice and oblation" subsequently is another way of recording that the brothers from Hexham would say their daily office of prayer as well as celebrate the Eucharist at this place.

Such was the prelude to the battle of Heavenfield which took place in 634. In this battle, the Anglo-Saxon Christian King Oswald of Northumbria defeated the Welsh King Cadwalla at Heavenfield, near Chollerford and Hexham, thus ending the possibility of Welsh pagan reconquest in the north and ensuring the triumph of Christianity in Northumbria. Here at the place called "heavenly field," and where the heavenly sign (of the cross) is set up at the very spot where Oswald has led them in prayer for the people, Bede remarks, there is a heavenly victory and heavenly miracles occur. Here Bede's sense of national destiny is stretched to its limits as the Northumbrians, who have adopted the Celtic (not Roman) form of Christianity, pray to the "almighty, everliving, and true God" to defend the nation. Their victory recorded here seems to suggest that even the staunchly pro-Roman Bede is not willing to write off non-Roman Christians as fit recipients of God's blessing with regard to the English nation and what he believes to be God's destiny for it. The entire context of the battle as well as the continuing prominence of the cross in works of healing at the end of this chapter suggest parallels to the stories of the "true cross" that emanated from Constantine's vision and victory at the Milvian Bridge in the fourth century. All of this Bede would presumably have known from the Latin translation of the history of Eusebius that was in circulation at that time.

Book III.3

Oswald's sending to Ireland for a bishop may seem strange since the bishop is Anglo-Saxon, but it makes more sense in that he was baptized under the Celtic bishops and had lived in Ireland for some seventeen years, primarily with the Celtic monks at Iona. So, when the king is in need of spiritual help, Oswald sends there for a bishop and receives Aidan, who had come to Lindisfarne from Iona in 635 and who turns out to be a strong missionary and an ideal bishop in Bede's eyes (save for his Celtic customs). That Aidan had "a zeal for God though not entirely according to knowledge" (cf. Romans 10:1-4) may well be indicative of Bede's view of the Celtic Christians who, he believes, labor under a grievous burden of ignorance by observing Easter at the wrong time. Anatolius, whose treatise on Easter based on a nineteen-year cycle which "the northern province of the Irish and the whole nation of the Picts" think they are following, had been Bishop of Laodicea and died about the year 282; his writing would surface again in the disputes at Whitby (see below at III.25).

The king appointed Aidan to be the bishop of Lindisfarne, an island off the northeast coast of Britain that has been known from the eleventh century as "Holy Island." Celtic missionaries and saints loved to select remote, beautiful, inaccessible places such as this to be their headquarters. "As the tide ebbs and flows, this place is surrounded twice daily by the waves of the sea like an island and twice, when the shore is left dry, it becomes again attached to the mainland," Bede wrote, and this is still an accurate description of the place, even though today there is also a modern causeway. The Anglican parish church on Lindisfarne is thought to stand upon, and to incorporate portions from, the seventh-century monastic church founded there by Aidan himself. There are also an exhibition center, a retreat center, and a modern ecumenical community called Marygate House, as well as a very fine website.

We note that the itinerant preacher-priests who are sent out into Oswald's kingdom from Lindisfarne are said to baptize and to instruct in the Word, but Bede does not record their celebration of the Mass (possibly because the celebration of this sacrament was reserved for clergy following the Roman use). It is noteworthy that it is the king who interprets Aidan's preaching to the thegns and ealdormen (senior members of the royal court), since Bishop Aidan himself is "not completely at home in the English tongue." That the king gave "lands and property to establish monasteries" and also "gave Aidan a place for his episcopal see" on Lindisfarne, indicates the close relationship of church and state in this period.

Book III.4

Bede now steps back in time a bit in order to present the parallel fortunes of two ecclesiastical notables from Northumbria, Ninian and Columba. St. Ninian in the fifth century was the first bishop at Candida Casa (Latin for "The White House," so called from the white stone of which its church, dedicated to St. Martin of Tours, was constructed), which was later known as Whithorn in Galloway (cf. V.23). We know little more about Ninian other than that he preached the gospel among the southern Picts in the lowlands of southwest Scotland. Bede tells us, no doubt with approval, that Ninian had received instruction in Rome. His traditional feast day is September 16. The Pictish people we have already encountered at I.1 and I.12.

St. Columba (c. 521-597) went from Ireland to become the founder of the important monastery of Iona, a small island of the Inner Hebrides just off the west coast of Scotland. Iona became the earliest center of Celtic Christianity, known for its monastic life and missionary activity especially in the sixth century. Near Oban on the mainland, it is reached today by ferry from the island of Mull. Earlier it had been a center of Druidic sun-worship. St. Columba with his twelve companions built a monastery here that would develop the usual Celtic pattern, with its church and refectory of wood, a group of stone bee-hive huts, and an encircling wall for protection. Here they lived a hard, simple, austere life of prayer and praise, copying manuscripts, fishing, and sailing on missionary journeys among the Pictish peoples. This important monastery fostered the Celtic tradition, although keeping the wrong date of Easter (Bede tells us) "for a very long time, no less than 150 years, up to the year of our Lord 715." Columba is traditionally commemorated in liturgical calendars on June 9. The late-seventh-century *Life of Columba* by Adomnan is one of the few historical sources that Bede seems not to have known.

As the father/abbot of this entire community, Columba increasingly lived as a solitary and finally died in 597 at the age of seventy-six. Columba himself founded two monasteries and his disciples founded many others, which were linked together in some sort of federated arrangement whereby they were all dependent upon Iona itself; cf. III.21, V.9. Regarding Bede's statement that Iona "always has an abbot for its ruler who is a priest, to whose authority the whole kingdom, including even bishops, have to be subject," we should perhaps read his subsequent remark about "this unusual arrangement" as meaning "contrary to the Roman custom," which might have vested such supervisory authority in a bishop, although his remark may be intended to distinguish only those monasteries that were directly related to St. Columba. It is difficult to generalize about authority in Celtic monasteries in this period, although most Celtic bishops seem to have been non-diocesan and non-jurisdictional, and not all Celtic monasteries followed the Columban pattern.

Book III.5

Aidan, like Augustine, Chad, and Cuthbert, is one of Bede's model bishops. For more on Aidan, cf. III.14-17. Although a figure of great significance, Aidan was not particularly well chronicled, and Bede is the lone source of nearly all the extant information regarding Aidan. In this chapter Bede provides something just short of a checklist of qualifications for a model bishop in his view. Like Aidan, all model bishops should generally hold all goods in common, readily give to the poor, travel on foot, and be prepared to speak to anyone whether high or low — all of course after the example of the apostles (cf. I.26; III.14, 28; IV.3, 27). Much of the substance of this ideal seems to have come from St. Gregory the Great, and preference for travel by foot was also seen in that time as a sign of humility, of earthiness, and of scriptural fidelity (cf. Matthew 10:14; Luke 9:2-5; Luke 10:9-11; Acts 13:51). Riding on horseback, by contrast, was generally reserved to the upper classes. The Christian custom of fasting on Wednesdays and Fridays goes back to the early church, and "the ninth hour" indicates the prayer that was offered at the ninth hour of the sun-filled day, or about 2:30-3:00 P.M.

One of the most telling observations indicative of Bede's disapproval of what he seems to regard as a recent relaxation of spiritual standards is also found in this chapter, where Bede observes that Aidan's life was "in great contrast to our modern slothfulness." Bede goes on to lament that monks no longer read the Scriptures and memorize the Psalms the way they did during Aidan's lifetime. To put Bede's perennial complaint about the modern generation into some perspective, though, it is worth noting that Bede was born scarcely more than twenty years after Aidan's death.

Book III.6

In King Oswald, Bede here sets forth a model of humility in Christian kingship, not least for emulation by Ceolwulf, King of Northumbria and subsequently a monk of Lindisfarne, to whom Bede's *History* is dedicated in its Preface. Since Aidan was a model bishop, it is no surprise that those under his tutelage, such as Oswald, would prosper. Cf. III.14, III.22. There is also some correlation, Bede suggests, between the large size of Oswald's earthly kingdom and the kingdom of heaven for which he hopes, evidenced here and now by the story of the incorruptibility of Oswald's hand and arm, understood in the piety of the day as being attestations of holiness of life.[17]

---

17. For the dispersal and veneration of Oswald's remains, see the handlist compiled by John Blair near the end of Alan Thacker and Richard Sharpe, eds., *Local Saints and Local Churches in the Early Medieval West* (Oxford: Oxford University Press, 2002), pp. 549-50.

Book III.7

The Gewisse mentioned in the first line of this chapter are the West Saxons, the people of Wessex. Birinus was consecrated in Italy as a missionary bishop who at first operated without any fixed see. Bede tells us that Birinus was consecrated at the Pope's command by Asterius, the bishop of Genoa, but Asterius was really archbishop of Milan and merely resided in Genoa. St. Birinus eventually became the first bishop of Dorchester (some nine miles from Oxford) and died around the year 650. His feast day is traditionally observed on either 3 or 5 December. Although the activities ascribed to Birinus here are not up to the level of Bede's model bishops, Bede's treatment of him is positive overall. The Latin text specifies font-baptism, as is indicated in the Penguin edition, although not in the Oxford.

Cenwealh's rejection of Christianity results in the predictable losses of power and prestige which in Bede's narrative always accompany such actions. Bede's account of Cenwealh embraces a dogma of retribution (that bad deeds will be punished and good ones rewarded), but on the whole Cenwealh seems to do good after he has done wrong. Refusing to accept the faith and sacraments, he repudiated his wife and took another woman and lost his kingdom, but subsequently after exile he converts, accepts baptism, and is restored to his kingdom. The variations of ecclesiastical leadership described in this chapter are complex, but from Bede's account, it does seem that Wine, driven from his see as bishop of Winchester, actually purchased the bishopric of London from King Wulfhere. Such a transaction by purchase or sale of spiritual things, called "simony" (after the sin of Simon Magus in Acts 8:18-24), was not unknown at that time but was always opposed by the church.

Book III.8

We are now in the middle of the seventh century, and Bede obviously believes that the conversion of the nation has made great progress, Eorcenberht being "the first English king to order idols to be abandoned and destroyed throughout the whole kingdom."

The mention of "the brothers of the monastery who were in other buildings" calls to our attention the existence of so-called "double monasteries" that were not uncommon in Anglo-Saxon England. These were primarily nunneries ruled by abbesses (often of royal descent), with the male monks living separately at the same place and providing such functions as protection, education, and celebration of the sacraments. These so-called double monasteries were not exclusively English (the concept and pattern came from Gaul), although many of the most celebrated ones were English, such as Barking, Coldingham, Ely, Whitby, and Wimborne. These double monasteries were at their zenith in England during the seventh century, but declined after the Danish, Scandinavian invasions of the ninth and tenth centuries. See Bede, Books III.11, IV.7, and IV.25 for other examples.[18]

It is not unusual in this period to find reports that the bodies of holy persons, when their tombs were opened, were found to be incorrupt and exuding a sweet smell. One such, which Bede records here, was Ethelberga (spelled "AEthelburh" in the Oxford text), who had been abbess of Faremoutier-en-Brie (near Meaux in France); other examples are found in Bede at III.19, IV.19, and IV.30. This phenomenon is seldom reported in western churches today, but it is frequently claimed in the Orthodox Church of Russia as an indication of probable sainthood.

Book III.9-10

Chapter 9 begins with an ironic second mention of the removal of apostate kings from historical memory, which was recounted earlier in III.1. Bede's effort to praise such a revision only reiterates what common consent had agreed to forget. Oswald fell in battle, killed by Penda of Mercia in 642 at Maserfelth (Maserfield, probably Oswestry, "Oswald's Tree or Cross," in Shropshire), dissolving Northumbria into two separate kingdoms, Bernicia and Deira. The miracles attributed to Oswald continue to spring from the

---

18. Further see Deanesly, *The Pre-Conquest Church,* pp. 199-202; and C. J. Godfrey, *The Church in Anglo-Saxon England* (Cambridge: Cambridge University Press, 1962), pp. 157-59.

very ground on which he died, chapter 10 being merely an extension of the previous. Wallace-Hadrill observes that Oswald's miraculous powers are here extended to a British traveler, who was not one of Oswald's former subjects. This extension is noteworthy as it indicates the belief that God's power in the spiritual domain was not limited to the purely geographical domain formerly ruled by Oswald. St. Oswald today is commemorated in the calendar of the Church of England on August 5.

Book III.11

The story of Oswald's bones and how they were left outside has a life beyond the pages of Bede's *History*. The reference to the king's bones remaining outside these gates all night, indicated by a pillar of light, gave rise to the tradition that hereafter the monks of Bardney never again closed their doors by day or night and that in Lincolnshire persons coming from Bardney could be recognized because they habitually left their doors open (or at least unlocked) even at night.

When speaking of the location where the water was poured within which the bones of Oswald had been washed, the Latin text *in angulo sacrarii* is rendered "in the corner of the cemetery" by the Penguin edition while the Oxford translation reads "in a corner of the sanctuary." The latter is regarded as probably correct. The exorcism, which occurs later in the chapter with assistance from a relic of Oswald, confirms that Bardney was a double monastery, for a priest from the men's quarter does the sacramental ministration; cf. III.8.

Book III.12

The boy suffering from a disease which the Oxford translation calls "recurrent fevers" and the Penguin edition renders "ague" probably had symptoms similar to malaria. This boy is healed by sustained physical proximity to King Oswald's tomb in a process similar to that known as "incubation" in some of the Orthodox churches of the East from very early times. Professor

Margaret Deanesly comments: "The veneration for a saint's relics goes back to the early days of Christianity, to the days of the martyrs in particular. The Christian teaching that those who died in Christ lived in him was vividly held, so that for the Christian there was no such thing as annihilation in death: the dead in Christ lived on and aided the living by their prayers. Those whom they had loved and helped in life they continued to love and help after death: prayer by their relics, or objects associated with them, was efficacious prayer and would certainly obtain the help of God."[19] It is noteworthy that Oswald's customary posture for prayerful meditation was sitting, "his hands on his knees with the palms turned upwards." Bede remarks: "It is not to be wondered at that the prayers of this king who is now reigning with the Lord should greatly prevail, for while he was ruling over his temporal kingdom, he was always accustomed to work and pray most diligently for the kingdom which is eternal."

Penda, the pagan King of Mercia, had ordered that Oswald's body be severed into pieces. His head was soon placed in the shrine of St. Cuthbert at Lindisfarne, some of his bones went to Bardney (see III.11, above), and some of his relics were taken to Frisia (cf. III.13). Oswald's head was eventually (re)discovered in 1827 when the coffin of St. Cuthbert was opened.[20]

Book III.13

Acca was bishop of Hexham from 709-31 and a disciple of Wilfrid whom he succeeded as bishop there (cf. V.20, below). The holiness of King Oswald has already worked miracles and is now spreading, as Wilfrid and Acca, journeying to Rome, stop for a time with Willibrord, "archbishop of the Frisians." The latter was a native Northumbrian who had been educated under Wilfrid at Ripon where Wilfrid had been abbot. On this journey they learn of still another miracle of healing, associated with a relic of Oswald and a promise to submit to God in return. It is the story of a man

19. Deanesly, *The Pre-Conquest Church*, pp. 75-76.
20. C. F. Battiscombe, ed., *The Relics of St. Cuthbert* (Oxford: Oxford University Press, 1956), pp. 5, 96.

who was healed by drinking some water in which a portion of the stake that held the head of St. Oswald had been placed (for a parallel, see III.2 above).

Willibrord speaks of himself early in this chapter as "living a pilgrim's life in Ireland out of love for his eternal fatherland," a typical description of the early English Christian view of life in which we are all pilgrims and wanderers in journey towards our heavenly home. Early Irish monks were said sometimes to take to sea in rudderless boats and then to land and evangelize and settle wherever God seemed to direct. The land that Bede refers to as Frisia is now part of the Netherlands and northwest Germany.

Book III.14

Here begins a period of "twenty-eight troubled years," as Bede describes the reign of Oswiu, Oswald's brother. About the same time, Bishop Paulinus, of York and then of Rochester, also dies (644). Paulinus was buried probably in the "sanctuary" of the church of St. Andrew at Rochester, the Latin word *secretarium* being correctly translated here "sanctuary" but wrongly translated as "sacristy" in the Penguin text and also now correctly translated as "sanctuary" in both Oxford and Penguin editions at II.1. Further on this intriguing problem of translation, see the comments at II.1.

Interest in this chapter focuses on the lives of, and relationship between, King Oswine and Bishop Aidan, who are models as king and bishop in Bede's view. Bede especially admires them for their humility, which in the view of early medieval theology was the virtue that could best correct the sin of pride. (Later, in the high Middle Ages and the time of St. Francis, this early medieval emphasis upon humility will be eclipsed by a redirection of emphasis upon the virtue of poverty as the way to overcome the sin of avarice that was becoming so rampant in an increasingly commercialized society.)

As a king, Oswine's life is marked by humility, impartiality, and concern for the welfare of his people. "Tall and handsome, pleasant of speech, courteous in manner, and bountiful to nobles and commons alike," Oswine seems equipped with a generous measure of personal charm. His apparently pragmatic decision not to do battle against the far stronger forces of his brother Oswiu seems to have precipitated his own personal exile and almost certainly allowed his treacherous murder by his brother in the year 651. Oswine is venerated as a saint on August 20.

Aidan, likewise, is one of Bede's model bishops, also displaying humility and a marked lack of concern for material things, as we have already seen in III.3 and III.5. Both these traits can be inferred from the story that Bede tells here of how Aidan gave away a prize horse, which was a personal gift from Oswine, to a beggar. Oswine had given Aidan the horse to allow Aidan to travel more quickly and easily when need pressed, but Bede is quick to affirm that "he was normally accustomed to walk" (as were all Bede's model bishops). Aidan for his part, we are told, was not corrupted by regard from people in power, as his principal concern always remained for the welfare of the poor. In the end, Aidan convinced the king to adopt this concern. Liturgically, St. Aidan is commemorated on August 31, the day of his death as recorded here by Bede.

Book III.15-16

As with King Oswald, Aidan's fame continues to spread after the news of his death has been told, and Bede in chapters 15-17 recounts evidence of three "miracles" attributed to Aidan (the Latin actually reads *miraculorum signis,* or "signs of miracles"). Bede opens chapter 15 with the statement that "He who judges the heart showed by signs and miracles what Aidan's merits were," which he thus presents as having an evangelistic purpose for the spread of the gospel.

Previously in Bede we have encountered sacramental uses of holy oil, but this is the first appearance of holy oil outside that context. One wonders, though, whether Bede would have regarded this particular use of holy oil, to quell the storm and the winds, as being non-sacramental. Bede's assessment of this miracle as recorded at the end of chapter 15 presents an interesting picture of how Bede treats his original materials, scrupulously recording the sources where he got his evidence. He notes that he has received this story from Cynemund, a faithful priest of his own church at Jarrow, who received it from the priest Utta who actually performed the miracle. Aidan died in 651, so it is quite likely that Utta had passed the story to

Cynemund or someone else who was still living when Bede was writing. (Bede's dates, we recall, were 672/3-735.)

The diversion of the flames recorded in chapter 16 comes closer to being the sort of natural event that modern readers might more easily allow to be called a "miracle," but in it also Bede gives a different and more nuanced picture of miracles. This time, rather than competing with the forces of nature as in the case of the oil poured on the sea in III.15, the miracle that Bede records in III.16 could easily indicate no more than the wind changing direction and saving the city from burning. To Bede, each is as convincing a testimony to Aidan's holiness as the other. We note that Aidan at this time had been living on nearby Farne Island, where "he often used to retire to pray in solitude and silence." This place would later be used by St. Cuthbert and others, and can still be visited today with only minimal physical discomfort but with great spiritual benefit.

Book III.17

The story of Aidan's death yields some insight about the living arrangements of kings and bishops in early England, for it indicates the close relationship between these two sorts of leaders as well as the peripatetic nature of their lives. Bede's observation that Aidan was staying "on a royal estate" where he had "a church and a cell where he often used to go and stay, . . . for he had no possessions of his own except the church and a small piece of land around it" is perhaps the most telling. Chronologically, Bede's records obviously do not extend into the later medieval period, when bishops themselves would have several manor houses where they would stay as they traveled.

The third miracle attributed to Aidan, after Bede has told his readers of the oil on the water and the diversion of the flames, is the indestructibility, even by fire and the threats of King Penda, of the pillar against which Aidan was leaning when he died. It has been suggested that this story of "Aidan's Pillar," for Christians, came to supersede the pagan story of "Thor's Pillar," and is thus an example of the triumph of Christian miracle over pagan miracle, but there seems little causal connection beyond similarity. Thor, the pagan god of thunderstorms, had a particularly close association with groves of oak trees, perhaps because of the dramatic sight produced when an oak was struck by lightning, and Thor's Pillar in Essex was regarded as a particularly vivid manifestation of Thor's presence.[21] Although there is little trace of any such place in modern guidebooks, the story itself does seem plausible, but there is little to suggest that the Christian story of Aidan's Pillar was invented by Christians to supplant Thor's Pillar. Insertion of woodchips in water recalls the stories we have already read in III.2 and III.13.

Bede's final evaluation of Aidan is quite commendatory, admitting Aidan's praiseworthy features as a "truthful historian" must do *(quasi verax historicus)*, and offering a long list of Aidan's admirable qualities, but nonetheless registering his strong disapproval of Aidan's Celtic observance of Easter. In spite of Aidan's failure to "observe Easter at the proper time," which Bede "heartily detests," Bede does emphasize his basic theological agreement with Aidan who, "in his celebration of Easter ... reverenced and preached no other doctrine than we do, namely the redemption of the human race by the passion, resurrection, and ascension into heaven of the one mediator between God and men, even the man Christ Jesus." The final lines of this chapter, in addition, record Aidan's conviction, from which Bede does not dissent, that the final resurrection, our own, will take place "on this same first day of the week now called the Lord's Day" (Sunday), a view shared by Gregory the Great and others.

Book III.18

For more on the life of Sigeberht, King of East Anglia, see II.15. He was the first Anglo-Saxon ruler to enter the religious life.[22] Every bit a Christian philanthropist in setting up schools to emulate those he had seen on the continent, Sigeberht's conversion to the religious life is quite complete and his zeal is unabated in his new endeavors. Adamant in his monastic vows at Bury St. Edmunds, Sigeberht is so opposed to violence that he must be

---

21. Henry Mayr-Harting, *The Coming of Christianity to Anglo-Saxon England* (University Park: Pennsylvania State University Press, 1972; 3rd ed. 1991), p. 27.

22. Godfrey, *Church in Anglo-Saxon England,* p. 99.

dragged out to the battlefield where he dies, unarmed and with nothing more than a stick, in a battle which he tried to avoid.

Book III.19

Here we have Bede's account of the life and visions of Fursa (also known as "Fursey"), a holy man from Ireland who is spending his life as a pilgrim, which was a not uncommon feature of the spiritual landscape of that time. The extent to which such persons and tales about such persons were taken quite seriously at that time, albeit often mixtures of fact and fantasy, can be seen from the seriousness with which Bede treats the accounts of Fursa's peregrinations. Always the careful historian, though, Bede records here only one incident from a little book about Fursa and leaves the other accounts for his readers to investigate if they are interested. Fursa's fiery out-of-body experiences in a few instances seem to parallel some of the fourth-century imagery of St. Athanasius' *Life of Antony,* who, like Fursa, also had an out-of-body experience and was led by angel escorts through a pack of demonic accusers. There is a short, anonymous "life" of Fursa that is extant, but not in English translation, and manuscripts of his visions were popular reading in the Middle Ages. We note that here in chapter 19, as always, Bede is careful to use the Latin *altare* when he is referring to a Christian altar but not for a pagan one, which would be *ara* (cf. I.7 and II.13).

Book III.20

"Gyrwe" was a collective name for a small number of related groups in this part of the country. Chapter 20 recounts the succession of a series of less notable bishops, and it is not entirely clear how many bishops were present for each of these consecrations that Bede notes (cf. I.27, question 6, but also see II.4). Thomas, who became bishop of the East Angles 648-653, and about whom very little is known, seems to have been consecrated directly to the episcopate from the diaconate. Deusdedit was the first Anglo-Saxon to be made archbishop of Canterbury. The care with which such historical episcopal successions are recorded in Bede, obviously stemming from the Roman sense of order and centralized authority but of rather less concern in Celtic understanding, is a noteworthy feature that the Church of England and other Anglican churches stemming from it still have in common with the Roman Catholic even down to the present.

Book III.21

Peada's conversion as described in this chapter seems to have been more political than spiritual in character, and is clearly related to the promise he makes to Oswiu (also known as "Oswy") that he and his people will accept the Christian faith in return for the hand of Oswiu's daughter given to him in marriage. Peada's father, King Penda, is now less hostile than previously, and some limited comparison can be made between his attitude and the toleration policy of King Ethelbert in I.26 above, although Bede reports that Penda most of all detests insincerity. The place of Peada's baptism (by St. Finan) was probably at Wallbottle, near Hadrian's Wall.

At the end of this chapter we read that it became necessary to consecrate Diuma as bishop both of the Middle Angles and of the Mercians, "since a shortage of bishops made it necessary for one bishop to be set over both nations." What is presented here by Bede as a matter of expedience seems to point to a deeper reality, namely, that at this time such bishops were more often seen as tribal rather than territorial or geographical. The Penguin at this point reads "shortage of priests," however, Bede's Latin being *paucitas sacerdotum,* but the Oxford translation makes more sense even though elsewhere in the very same chapter both the Oxford and the Penguin have been translating *sacerdos* as "priest," which is equally possible since at this period in history this particular word could mean either. See also V.9 below.

Book III.22

Throughout Bede's *History,* there is a sense that the national destiny is tied to the election of the English as a people of God. This theology underlies much of Bede's text. A particularly fine example of this theology, which is fundamentally rooted in the story of ancient Israel, can be seen here in Oswiu's description of the true God to Sigeberht, King of the East Saxons. (This is not the Sigeberht, King of East Anglia, of whom we have read in II.15 and III.18.) Oswiu's reasoning to Sigeberht bears a striking similarity to Old Testament polemics against idolatry. Oswiu pointed out that "objects made by the hands of men could not be gods. Neither wood nor stone were materials from which gods could be created, the remnants of which were either burned in the fire or made into vessels for men's use or else cast out as refuse, trodden underfoot and reduced to dust." In contrast to these mere objects, Oswiu offers Sigeberht a vision of the one true God in whom Christians believe. This God is "incomprehensible in His majesty, invisible to human eyes, omnipotent, eternal, Creator of heaven and earth and of mankind, who rules over the world and will judge it in righteousness. We must believe that His eternal abode is in heaven, not in base and perishable metal." Given such clearly contrasting options, it is hardly surprising that Sigeberht and his advisors become convinced and are baptized, probably at the same place and time as Peada, probably on the royal estate at Wallbottle near Hadrian's Wall.

After his conversion at Oswiu's court, Sigeberht returns home. He sends immediately for teachers to instruct the inhabitants of his kingdom in the Christian faith. Cedd, who was brought up with his brother St. Chad at Lindisfarne under St. Aidan, successfully evangelizes the East Saxons, teaching, converting, and baptizing throughout the kingdom. Cedd is in turn consecrated bishop of the East Saxons in 654 by St. Finan, a Celtic monk who had succeeded St. Aidan as bishop of Lindisfarne, together with two other consecrating bishops. Although consecration by only one bishop was the Celtic custom, we recall that consecration by three was the canonical number stipulated by the first council of Nicaea in 325 (cf. I.27 above, question 6, and III.28 below). Cedd as a bishop now proceeds to ordain both priests and deacons, thus continuing the three orders of ministry that have been constant in the church since the second and third centuries. Bede here mentions Ythancaestir, the old Roman fort of Othona, Essex, within the boundaries of which still stands the mid-seventh-century church of Bradwell-on-Sea (Essex).

Bede's retribution theology, the view that God rewards good deeds but punishes those who are not on his side, becomes somewhat more complex with the murder of King Sigeberht by his own kinsmen. Sigeberht, Bede tells us, made the mistake of dining with a nobleman *(gesith)* who had been excommunicated by Cedd because of an illicit marriage. Although Sigeberht repented, Cedd had pronounced that the very house of the nobleman where Sigeberht had dined would be the place of Sigeberht's death, and Bede tells us that this is exactly what happened. When Sigeberht is murdered two things may be observed. The first is Sigeberht's holiness, as he was killed for seeming to be too lenient towards his enemies — another of Bede's examples of royal humility such as we have already seen in Oswald and Oswine (III.6, III.14). The second observation is that Cedd's prophetic word is confirmed, which indicates the seriousness of excommunication and the perception of the spiritual authority of bishops in Bede's day. Nor does Bede conceal his admiration for Sigeberht, who was killed because "he was too ready to pardon his enemies, calmly forgiving them for the wrongs they had done," his death being because "he had devoutly observed the gospel precepts."

Book III.23

The royal foundation of monasteries by grants of land had at its base a belief in the efficacy of the prayers of the faithful on behalf of their ruler, and that by such prayers the kingdom itself would prosper. King Ethelwald ("Oethelwald") in 659 grants Cedd the land for the monastery of Lastingham (near Whitby) because Ethelwald "firmly believed that the daily prayers of those who served God there would greatly help him." Cedd's choice of place "amid some steep and remote hills" is typical of Celtic monks, as was his desire "first of all to cleanse the site from the stain of former crimes by prayer and fasting." Such behavior was the customary Celtic way to dedicate a sacred site, and it was this Celtic usage from Lindisfarne, where Cedd had been trained, that Cedd brought to Lastingham and also shared in common with his brother Chad. This Celtic tradition of purifying the site of a future monastery or church by a period of prayer and fasting at the place was observed here over the entire season of Lent, Bede tells us.

At the end of this chapter we read of Cedd's death at Lastingham in 664, and a group of monks from Cedd's former monastery in the kingdom of the East Saxons come to Lastingham to be near the remains of their spiritual father. Sadly, all of them seem to have contracted the same plague there that was responsible for Cedd's demise, except for one young boy, who fell ill with the rest but recovered and was baptized and subsequently ordained. We note that Cedd bequeathed the abbacy of the Lastingham monastery to his brother Chad, a practice of hereditary transfer that was common at the time but not universally approved. Lastingham, located near an old Roman road, still boasts a church of the eleventh century with a very interesting crypt, in which is an altar upon which Chad is thought to have possibly celebrated Mass.

Book III.24

King Penda of Mercia is finally defeated by King Oswiu of Northumbria at the battle of the Winwood ("Winwaed") River in 654-655. The theological basis of King Oswiu's vow to dedicate his year-old daughter to a monastery in perpetual virginity, in addition to illustrating the practice of child-oblation common at that time, says much about the very close relations between the church and the state then as well as about Bede's confidence in the destiny of England as a Christian nation. These monasteries of royal foundation, which were part of the king's vow, were free from any obligation to offer military support to the king but only prayers, inasmuch as upon their territories "heavenly warfare" was to be waged in place of "earthly military service," and the monks were to "pray with unceasing devotion" for the "eternal peace" of the nation. Streaneshalch (as it is called in Bede's text) was located on the coast of North Yorkshire. Later named Whitby by the Danes, it was one of the "double monasteries" for monks and nuns discussed above at III.8, and Hilda was to become its most famous abbess. The location of Winwaed is uncertain, but it is suggested to be a tributary of the Humber River.

Oswiu and his small army are said to have gone into battle against im-

possible odds, while "trusting in Christ their leader." The origins of this battle have been clouded by time and even Bede's text is not exactly precise regarding who is responsible for the war between Oswiu and Penda, nor is the
confusion helped by Bede's account of Penda's apparent conversion back in
III.21. If Penda were still a pagan, the report of his defeat in Bede would at
least make theological sense. Also complicating matters is Bede's silence
about the revolt against Oswiu in South Mercia, which does not seem to
bother Bede since all the parties to the revolt still regard Christ as their true
King. This willingness to overlook rebellion against a Christian king
(Oswiu) suggests that Bede did not envision any one particular civil government as being exclusively the instrument of God.

Ever since the victory of Oswiu over Penda at the battle of the
Winwood River in 654-655, it is said that no English ruler has been openly
identified with an anti-Christian policy. It has been remarked that before
the death of Penda Christians were too preoccupied over the struggle with
paganism for there to be any effective unification of the Celtic and Roman
strands of Christianity, but that now this becomes at least possible and the
road to Whitby (chapter 25) is open. Deanesly, however, cautions against
assuming that "England" was already "Christian" at the time of Whitby, for
there had been relapses to paganism at the East Anglian and East Saxon
courts after Ethelbert's death in 616, and the great pagan ship-burial at
Sutton Hoo took place in nominally Christian East Anglia just on the eve
of the 664 Whitby synod, while in the rest of the Anglo-Saxon territories
conversion had hardly begun.[23]

Book III.25

This chapter contains Bede's account of the Synod of Whitby, which was
held in 664. Bede understandably sees this chapter, placed as it is at the very
center of his book and of the history he is writing, as celebrating the fulfill-
ment of Pope Gregory's mission to England, the pledge of unity for the nation based upon a common liturgy, the promise that diversity will be

23. Deanesly, *The Pre-Conquest Church,* p. 61.

checked by centripetal motion, and the certainty that henceforth the Church in England will soon be united in a common observance of a common date for celebration of the most important Christian feast, visibly and sacramentally linked by its episcopal structure in communion with the wider church.

Disputes over the correct calculation of the date on which to commemorate the most important celebration in the Christian year, the Easter feast of the Lord's resurrection, already went back more than three hundred years, at least to the time of the first ecumenical council of Nicaea in 325, and their detail cannot be simplified adequately for the purpose of these notes.[24] It was logical for a Christian ruler of a Christian kingdom to seek to heal a division of his subjects on a major question like the date of Easter. King Oswiu at the beginning of Whitby in 664, somewhat like the Emperor Constantine at the beginning of the council of Nicaea, now urges that all who serve the same one God should observe the same rule and therefore should not differ in celebrating the sacraments of heaven on earth, inasmuch as they all hope for the same one heavenly kingdom.

The debates at Whitby were conducted between Colman, bishop and abbot of Lindisfarne, representing the Celtic tradition that had come by way of Iona and Ireland from the north, and Wilfrid, abbot of Ripon and later archbishop of York, representing the Roman tradition of Christianity that had come from the southeast by means of St. Augustine who had been sent to England by Pope Gregory the Great. (Cuthbert, it seems, was not there.) Very perceptive explanations of the immediate points at issue here, and especially of the Paschal controversy over the date of Easter, are found in the remarks of J. Campbell appended near the end of this *Companion* and also in chapter 7 of Henry Mayr-Harting, *The Coming of Christianity to Anglo-Saxon England.* The debates at Whitby focused upon the correct calculation for the date of Easter and the correct form of clerical tonsure, the underlying question being whether the kingdom was to continue to allow

---

24. The major source for the Easter decision taken by the first ecumenical council of Nicaea in 325 is Eusebius' *Life of Constantine,* III.18. A good summary of the issues and subsequent historical development can be found in *The Oxford Dictionary of the Christian Church,* under the heading of "Paschal Controversies."

the divergent Celtic ways or to be united under an allegiance to the Church of Rome. The Celtic argument, upheld by Colman and supported by Abbess Hilda and her community, focused on antiquity and decentralized authority, whereas the Roman argument, championed by Wilfrid, called for universality, discipline, and an understanding of doctrinal development under centralized, international leadership.[25]

Here at the Synod of Whitby, then, the Roman form of Christianity thus meets the Celtic head-on, and the triumph of Roman Christianity over Celtic is sealed at Whitby as the English Church is formally united by the decision of King Oswiu of Northumbria in favor of Rome. Bede, who stands clearly on the Roman side even though he admires the simplicity and poverty and individual examples of holiness seen in the Celts, understandably makes this event, this synod, the pivotal turning-point of his entire *History*. He may have over-emphasized the decisive finality of Whitby, though, and it is possible that the lines between "Celt" and "Roman" were not as finely drawn as his account suggests. Today, some historians even urge that at Whitby there was not really a "triumph" of one side at all, nor a "defeat" of the other.

We note that Bede, as author of such works as *De Temporum Ratione* and *De Temporibus,* does have a technical interest in the chronological dispute about the dating of Easter. The other major surviving account of the Whitby synod is in Eddius's *Life of Wilfrid* (printed in the Penguin paperback *Lives of the Saints,* ed. J. F. Webb; in *The Age of Bede,* ed. D. H. Farmer; and also in *Anglo-Saxon Saints and Heroes,* ed. C. Albertson). Both Bede and Eddius are favorable to the Roman point of view, but Eddius had more sympathy for the Celts than did Bede. Not only did the time seem "ripe" now for this confrontation at Whitby (see the comments above, at III.24), but the state of affairs had now gotten to the point that "it sometimes happened that Easter was celebrated twice in the same year, so that the king had finished the fast and was keeping [Celtic] Easter Sunday, while the queen and her people were still in Lent and observing [Roman] Palm Sunday"!! Bede does not attempt to disguise his own conviction, as he makes reference

25. The problem of doctrinal development and historical process can also be seen in Bede himself, below at IV.5 and 17.

to "the true Easter," and "the true and catholic Easter." The issues were far-reaching and with good reasons on both sides, but as regards the technical dispute noted at the end of this chapter over what had been written by Anatolius (bishop of Laodicea, who wrote a treatise on the date of Easter and died about the year 282), it does seem that the interpretation of Wilfrid was correct and that of Colman in error.[26]

Was the decision of Whitby a mistake, a sellout to size and organization, over the things of the Spirit? The great historian of the pre-reformation church in England, the Anglican bishop J. R. H. Moorman, concluded: "Either the English Church was to be brought into line with Western Christendom, or it was to struggle on in its independence. Had the Synod of Whitby chosen the latter course nothing but stagnation could have ensued. But by choosing in favour of Rome, the Church in England brought herself in touch with the blood-stream of the Catholic Church and could henceforth play her full part in the life of Christendom."[27] An earlier historian, J. L. G. Meissner, opined as follows: "The Celtic Church possessed undoubted zeal, enthusiasm, and learning, but in the sense of order and authority it was deficient. The latter qualities were the special legacy left by the representatives of the Roman Church."[28] A good question for discussion and reflection, as one reads Bede's account, is to ask whether one agrees with Moorman in his evaluation of the choice for Rome made by Oswiu on behalf of the English Church at Whitby. Perhaps a more pointed question is to ask whether one agrees with the decision of King Oswiu at the chapter's end, that a Christian is "committing sin" if he or she refuses to follow "the decrees of the apostolic see or rather of the universal Church" by preferring the teaching of the Celtic fathers, "a handful of people in one corner of the remotest of islands," over "the universal Church of Christ which is spread throughout the world," thus presuming to side with Columba over Peter and thus relegating England to continued life in an ecclesiastical backwater.

26. Cf. Deanesly, *The Pre-Conquest Church*, p. 87, and Book III.3 above.

27. J. R. H. Moorman, *A History of the Church in England* (London: A. & C. Black, 1980), p. 21.

28. J. L. G. Meissner, *The Celtic Church in England after the Synod of Whitby* (London: Hopkinson, 1929), pp. viii-ix.

A brief digression, or rather an extension of interpretations of Whitby into modern controversies over the very substance of Christian spirituality, is appropriate at this point. Arthur Holder, a contemporary Anglican historian of that subject, endorses the view by which Whitby is seen by many today as being the fulcrum of two very different approaches to Christian life, remarking that "the Irish missionaries from Iona, led by St. Aidan, had brought a form of Christianity that affirmed the goodness of creation, encouraged individual freedom of expression, fostered women's leadership, respected native indigenous traditions, and enjoyed the charismatic vitality of saintly wonder-workers while keeping bishops on hand for necessary sacramental functions. By contrast, the Roman missionaries from Augustine of Canterbury on down were authoritarian bureaucrats, obsessed with controlling sin and imposing order to the *n*th degree."[29] Anglican writers in the centuries after Whitby have rendered either positive or negative evaluations of that event, depending upon whether the "Roman" values of unity and centralization and hierarchical authority that it is thought to have affirmed are evaluated positively, or whether the "Celtic" values of diversity and freedom and so-called "creation-centered spirituality" that it is thought to have suppressed are considered to be more desirable, or vice versa. And which of these clusters of values, which of these emphases, whether Celtic or Roman, is more natural to the "spirit of Anglicanism," remains an ongoing subject of debate, just as the question of which approach is more true to the ideal of patristic Christian antiquity or to the necessity of the Christian future.

Bede has never left us in doubt as to where he stands, though. From the very opening of III.25 he tells us of the alterations to the new church on Lindisfarne, initially built by the (Celtic) Bishop Finan "after the Irish method, not of stone but of hewn oak, thatching it with reeds," but later under Archbishop Theodore (sent from Rome, we are reminded in IV.1) having

---

29. Arthur G. Holder, "Whitby and All That: The Search for Anglican Origins," *Anglican Theological Review* 85, no. 2 (Spring 2003): 237; this very perceptive article attempts to be fair to differing viewpoints. A 1987 book by Shirley Toulson, *The Celtic Alternative: A Reminder of the Christianity We Lost* (London: Rider, 1987), by its very title aptly summarizes one point of view, and a kindred approach is found in the work of Philip Newell, *Listening for the Heartbeat of God* (New York: Paulist, 1997). A helpful summary is Donald E. Meek, *The Quest for Celtic Christianity* (Edinburgh: Handsel Press, 2000).

been rededicated in honor of the blessed Apostle Peter and upgraded to a more substantial and sturdier structure with sheets of lead. Ever so subtle, the point is made that a church built on a firm foundation is also one that is under the protection of the Prince of the Apostles.

Agreeing with Bede from a Roman Catholic perspective, the late Cardinal Basil Hume of Westminster in 1996 offered a judicious if not unexpected evaluation of Whitby when he opined that "The Church must have authority, for whatever people may say we cannot live without it. . . . It is only through Peter, the guardian of the gates of heaven, that we can have a guarantee and protection of the faith we have. . . . The Synod of Whitby united all of Christian England with the greater universal tradition of the Roman Church."[30] Many Anglicans might well agree with Hume today, whereas some in his own church and many Protestants of various sorts might now give a greater weight to the "Celtic" values of diversity and freedom and flexibility of structure, as rightly or wrongly they see them. Both emphases are found in most churches today, and many would prefer not to have to choose one over the other.

After Whitby, Colman and many followers now gradually make their way from Lindisfarne first to Iona and then on to Inishboffin off the west coast of Ireland (cf. Book IV.4), as Celtic peculiarities and particularities gradually recede. Bede himself says very little of the conversion of Wales or Ireland, and nothing of St. David or St. Patrick or Armagh, his major theme being the gradual triumph and spread of Roman Christianity in England. The outlying regions were generally the last to accept the Roman ways, and the Celtic traditions in north Ireland, Wales, Devon, and Cornwall did not finally meet their demise until about the tenth century — all of which is a fascinating subject for research. For further spread of the Roman calculation of Easter and the Roman way of tonsure, and the eclipse of Celtic ways after Whitby, one may look to Book V.15, 18, 21, and also to the *Life of Wilfrid* by Eddius mentioned earlier. It is even held by some that the high crosses of Ruthwell and Bewcastle in the north of the country, as evidenced by the inscriptions upon them, were erected in the eighth century to com-

---

30. Basil Hume, *Footprints of the Northern Saints* (London: Darton, Longman & Todd, 1996), pp. 41-42, as excerpted in Holder, "Whitby and All That," p. 243.

memorate the decision of Whitby. Celtic influence continued, nonetheless, beyond Whitby and even on the continent, and could still be seen in such areas as monastic life, handwriting, private penance, and in sporadic manifestations of unrelenting independence that have never been subdued.

Book III.26

There had also been no small argument at Whitby between the two sides in the controversy about the form of tonsure, or clerical haircut, as the beginning of chapter 26 indicates here, the clergy of the Roman obedience cutting a small circle of hair off the crown of the head and letting the rest grow long at the extremities in a circle all around, whereas the Celtic clergy are said to have shaved the front of their heads from ear to ear while letting the hair grow long on the top and back (although this interpretation is disputed).[31] Whatever the theological and historical reasons alleged for each style, these differences of haircut did allow anyone at a glance to perceive on which side allegiance was being given.

The confirmation of Roman over Celtic rites at the Synod of Whitby puts Bede, stridently pro-Roman as he is, in a position to be conciliatory to Colman and other Celtic clerics who refuse to accept the ruling. Bede carefully praises the elements of their practice and theology with which he can agree (such as poverty, simplicity, and frugality) without compromising his own clear theological preference for Rome.

We have read of Aidan's death in III.14-17 above, and here Bede tells us that Colman took a portion of Aidan's bones for burial in the sanctuary of the church at Lindisfarne where Aidan had been bishop before Finan and himself. The Latin word for "sanctuary" here is *secretarium,* as we have seen in II.1 and III.14 above, although earlier Penguin editions had translated it as "sacristy."

In his description of these Celtic monks at the end of this chapter Bede does not mention the Eucharist, possibly because of his own reservations about the Celtic liturgy (see II.2 and II.8). Evidently admiring their piety

31. See Daniel McCarthy, "On the Shape of the Insular Tonsure," *Celtica* 24 (2003): 140-67; also see below at IV.1.

and their discipline of abstinence, their sole concern being "to serve God and not the world, to satisfy the soul and not the belly," Bede remarks that "the priests and the clerics visited the villages for no other reason than to preach, to baptize, and to visit the sick, in brief to care for their souls." He reports that these visits were apparently well received and served to extend the cause of Christ, but the absence of any mention of the Eucharist here is still worthy of note. As Colman and his followers made off for Iona, it does seem that the Celtic liturgy now soon entered a process of Romanization after Whitby, the principal source being the document known as the "Stowe Missal" that probably dates in its original version from 792 to 812 and may indicate Celtic usages in transition during the later half of the seventh century.[32] From Bede's perspective, of course, a common liturgical usage, just like a common date of Easter, had the potential of unifying the English nation against a previous background of rampant and seemingly carefree diversity. Just like the Whitby decision itself, so also a common liturgy, in Bede's eyes, could and would enable the church in Britain to be one — not only in mystical, intangible ways, but also visibly.

Book III.27

It is unclear whether the eclipse Bede mentions in the opening lines of this chapter is seen by him as an omen, or a historically significant event included for the purpose of dating the plague, or both. Egbert's recovery and subsequent missionary activity, his regimen of prayer and fasting, and his vow to remain an exile, call to mind the ideal of Christians as pilgrims in a foreign land. Egbert eventually became a monk of Iona and died there in 729. April 24 is the traditional day for his liturgical commemoration. He is to be distinguished from the King Egbert whom we shall encounter in III.29.

---

32. Marion J. Hatchett, "The Eucharistic Rite of the Stowe Missal," in *Time and Community: In Honor of Thomas Julian Talley*, ed. J. Neil Alexander (Washington, D.C.: Pastoral Press, 1990), pp. 153-70, at p. 154. For an extensive and detailed survey of the developments of early English liturgy from Augustine to Bede, if now slightly dated, see G. G. Willis, *Further Essays in Early Roman Liturgy*, Alcuin Club Collections no. 50 (London: SPCK, 1968), pp. 191-226.

Book III.28

Wilfrid, abbot of Ripon, who had been the leading speaker for the Roman side at Whitby, is now sent to Compiègne in Gaul for episcopal consecration to the see of York in order to avoid consecration by the Celtic bishops, whose credentials and orthodoxy are still under suspicion. King Oswiu, however, impatient at Wilfrid's long absence from the country, sends Chad, the abbot of Lastingham (cf. III.23), to Canterbury for consecration to the same see. Archbishop Deusdedit of Canterbury, however, has recently died (in 664; cf. III.20 above), and so Chad is consecrated to York by Bishop Wine of the West Saxons (whose credentials are under suspicion for simony; cf. III.7). We do note that this consecration, like that of Wilfrid, is done with the assistance of two other bishops (cf. III.22), even if the circumstances and credentials do not always meet Bede's standards. Following after the decision at the Synod of Whitby, we can thus see the growing ascendancy of Roman customs and practices being gradually worked out in the interactions described within this chapter. Here as in other places in Bede such as the beginning of the next chapter, "Catholic" generally means "Roman." Bede's model bishops such as Chad, we again note, travel on foot and are tireless evangelists after the manner of the apostles.

Book III.29-30

It is interesting that Bede does not see fit to include here the parts of Pope Vitalian's letter to King Oswiu that had to do with "celebrating the true Easter uniformly throughout the whole world," either because he considers the Easter controversy now closed, or because he may consider the Pope's observations too technical in nature, or for some other reason. Inasmuch as Bede is firmly pro-Roman in his convictions, it seems unlikely that Bede would have omitted any new directives that the Pope had chosen to stipulate.

The entire context of this papal letter, however, is the request of Kings Oswiu and Egbert for papal consecration of their own choice as the next archbishop of Canterbury following the death of Archbishop Deusdedit in

664, and the Pope's response that, the one whom they had chosen having died, he knows of no other suitable person at the present but will look for someone appropriate. We note that the English crown has appealed to Rome in this situation, and we note the Pope's response that once he finds a suitable candidate he will instruct him and send him along to them. We note also that Bede does not object to this Roman assumption of authority, and indeed he takes it for granted. Clearly, the situation here is more primitive and much more nuanced than the practice of papal "provisions" or appointments to episcopal sees that would escalate greatly in the later medieval period in England, but it is also true that precedents were now being set for future claims — such as a special prerogative claimed by later Popes to "provide" a successor of their choice to a vacant see if the designated candidate actually died at the Roman court while waiting for consecration by the Pope. Also, the papal reply here includes a list of relics of saints that were being sent to England from Rome — a clear indication of the considerable regard in which such foci of devotion were held at that time among even the highest levels of ecclesiastical and civil authority.

Chapter 30 merely confirms that at this time the distinction between Christian and pagan in England was still very thin, and the "conversion of England" hardly complete. The chapter concludes with Bede's implicit message that it is better to die for Christian truth than to continue living in the midst of apostasy. Near the end of chapter 30 (as elsewhere in I.7 and II.13, above), the Latin word for "altar" is *ara,* Bede's standard word for a pagan altar, not a Christian one (which is *altare*).

Book IV

This book presents the revival and reform of the English Church under the great Archbishop Theodore of Tarsus, as well as the lives of Wilfrid and Cuthbert.

Book IV.1

Bede's account of the revival and reform of the English Church under Archbishop Theodore of Tarsus begins with a short review of events chronicled in III.29 ("briefly mentioned in the preceding book," as he says). After the death of Archbishop Deusdedit, the Augustinian succession at Canterbury had lapsed with the death of Wighard at the apostolic see and prior to his consecration. As remarked above, Pope Vitalian assumes it is his prerogative to choose a successor, and his first candidate is one named Hadrian, who declines out of modesty, objecting that there is another "much better fitted both by age and learning to undertake the office of bishop." Hadrian then suggests to the Pope a certain "Andrew," who on grounds of ill health is unable to accept the nomination. Hadrian's second suggestion to the Pope is Theodore, a sixty-six-year-old Greek monk from Tarsus in Cilicia (at the southeast corner of modern Turkey, then under Arab rule), who accepts even though he is not yet ordained to the minor rank of subdeacon (cf. I.27). Theodore of Tarsus is therefore chosen and consecrated by Pope Vitalian in Rome on Sunday March 26 in 668, and the succession at Canterbury will hereafter derive from Theodore and henceforth under papal appointment. The Pope also stipulates that Hadrian, who had been abbot of a monastery near Naples, will accompany Theodore to England and support his teaching there. They set off together for England on May 27, the eve of Pentecost, and soon Theodore will appoint Hadrian as abbot of the monastery of Sts. Peter and Paul (later St. Augustine's).

We note Bede's offhand mention of national origins, Hadrian being an African and Theodore an Asiatic Greek. Although Bede does not see the need to comment on their respective races, he does spend considerable time explaining how Pope Vitalian took steps to ensure that Theodore did not introduce "any Greek customs which might be contrary to the true faith." With one exception, Bede does not name what these "Greek customs" might be, but he does give us the clear sense that some differences, especially theological, were perceived between the Greek and the Roman churches. The one difference that is named is the matter of tonsure, for it is indicated that Theodore waited and let his hair grow out for four months after receiving the subdiaconate so that he could receive the Roman style of circular tonsure in the shape of a crown before he was consecrated as a bishop (cf. III.26). Whether he was ordained deacon and priest along the way, we are not told.

Hitherto, Bede tells us, Theodore had worn "the tonsure of the holy apostle Paul, after the Eastern manner," but there is much difference of opinion as to what this meant and whether Theodore was now being required to accept the western, and circular, tonsure because he was becoming a western bishop or because he was now being expected to look like a western (but not Celtic) monk. Some have reasoned, because Bede says that he waited four months for his hair to grow in order to receive the circular tonsure, that he must have previously worn an Eastern style of tonsure that consisted in shaving the entire head. Bede seems to describe this as "the tonsure of the holy apostle Paul" because in Acts 18:18 Paul had had his hair cut off at Cenchreae, presumably in obedience to the Nazirite vow referenced in Numbers 6:18. But whether the "Pauline" style described in Acts was "after the Eastern manner" at that time, as Bede implies, or really consisted in shaving the entire head, is uncertain. Nor is it fully known how a custom of shaving the entire head would have changed and developed into the rather ample hairstyle and beard that has come to characterize Eastern Orthodox monks and bishops of later centuries.[33] Lest all this concern about tonsures seem a bit overdone, though, we recall that the style of tonsure had been one of the issues in dispute at the Synod of Whitby, which occurred only some four years earlier (cf. III.26). That Theodore might have chosen or opted for the Celtic style of tonsure as a gesture of reconciliation or even

---

33. On styles of tonsure, see A. A. King, *Liturgies of the Past* (London: Longmans, Green and Co., 1959), pp. 198-99; F. E. Warren, *Liturgy and Ritual of the Celtic Church* (Oxford: Clarendon, 1881; 2nd ed. by J. Stevenson, 1987), pp. 67-68; McCarthy, "On the Shape of the Insular Tonsure"; Caitlin Corning, *The Celtic and Roman Traditions: Conflict and Consensus in the Early Medieval Church* (New York: Palgrave Macmillan, 2006), pp. 13-14; and above at III.26. Bede says nothing about Theodore's tonsure in his *Commentary on the Acts of the Apostles* (Cistercian Studies Series 117, Kalamazoo, Mich.: Cistercian Publications, 1989, p. 150), which was written between 709 and 716 and thus earlier than his *History*, although at the point of Acts 18:18 in that volume Bede does comment that Paul "played the part of a Jew himself in order to win over the Jews," which might be taken to imply that Theodore was now playing the part of a western monk in order to win over his new monastic community at Canterbury.

compromise between the Roman and Eastern styles, however, is not even mentioned as a possibility!

Book IV.2

Theodore, now about the age of sixty-six, arrives in England in the year 669, exactly one year after the date he set out. Accompanied by Hadrian, he immediately begins visiting, teaching, consecrating bishops, reorganizing dioceses, correcting abuses, and generally promoting ecclesiastical stability and unity. Bede's comment that Theodore was "the first of the archbishops whom the whole English Church consented to obey" can be taken to imply that a good measure of ecclesiastical unity was being achieved. "Never had there been such happy times since the English first came to Britain," Bede remarks, and recent studies have confirmed Bede's high estimate of his achievements.

Bede's observation that "the knowledge of sacred music, which had hitherto been known only in Kent, [now] began to be taught in all the English churches" has been linked to the development of plainsong music in the time of Pope Vitalian and also to the possibility of some kind of liturgical reform, although it has been suggested that the church music of seventh-century Rome probably differed very little from that of the Greek church in which Archbishop Theodore was brought up. James the Deacon was also instrumental in these developments (cf. II.20), as was Bishop Wilfrid.

Theodore in 669 also regularizes in some way Chad's earlier consecration (cf. III.28), recalling him from retirement at Lastingham and appointing him in 669 as Bishop of the Mercians with his see at Lichfield.

Book IV.3

In this chapter Bede continues the story from the end of the previous chapter, reviewing the life of St. Chad all the way to his death and burial, in the midst of plague. Chad's devotion to a simple life is again praised, and Bede carefully notes Chad's reluctance to ride horseback, even though Archbishop Theodore insists. Earlier Penguin editions read that Chad "received the Bishopric of Mercia and Lindisfarne," but this has now been corrected to "Bishopric of the Mercians and the people of Lindsey," and the Oxford text is very close: "bishop of the Mercian race and of the people of Lindsey."

The end of Chad's life shares a number of features common to medieval hagiography. There is an announcement that his death is drawing near, angelic voices are heard, and Chad commands that no one be told of the heavenly song, all being events that are paralleled in the lives of some other saints. (See also Book IV.14, 24, 29.) It is possible that the injunction to keep the impending death a secret may have been patterned on Jesus' command to "Tell no one the vision" as recorded in Matthew 17:9. We note that Chad prepares for death by receiving the consecrated Blood, as well as the Body, of the Lord, an explicit reference to communion in both kinds at a time when such dual reception is on the decrease in spite of the precedent inherited from the Last Supper.

Chad dies on 2 March 672, which is now widely kept as his feast day, and miracles of healing are soon reported from sleeping near his relics ("incubation," as in III.12) or drinking their dust mixed in water (cf. III.13, V.18). Chad's holiness of life, and by implication his worthiness as a model of life for other Christians, is attested by the miracles associated with his relics. The ancient shrine of St. Chad, which became the focus of subsequent veneration, was recently (2006) rediscovered by archaeologists during excavations underneath the floor of the nave of Lichfield Cathedral.[34]

Book IV.4

We have last seen Colman at the conclusion of the Synod of Whitby at the end of III.25 and beginning of III.26, and we now find him active in founding the island monastery of Inishboffin off the west coast of Ireland. Once again, there is a clash of customs between English monks who stay in seclusion and the Irish monks whose habits have traditionally included a sort of wandering evangelism. Colman finds a most expedient solution, and his

---

34. *Church of England Newspaper* no. 5809: March 3, 2006.

segregation of the two groups into two separate monasteries apparently solves the problem.

Book IV.5

Here Bede records King Oswiu's desire to make a pilgrimage to Rome, unfulfilled before his death at the age of fifty-eight. In fact, in this early period many English kings traveled to Rome as being the location of holy places, spiritual power, and a center of pilgrimage (see also IV.12, V.7, 9, 19). By contrast, it has been observed, after the late eleventh century Rome was being visited mainly as a center of ecclesiastical administration and governance.[35]

There has been disagreement among specialists as to whether the Synod of Hertford took place in 672 or 673, but what is generally accepted is that it (not Whitby) is to be reckoned as the first national synod of the English Church and that Archbishop Theodore presided over it. Churchmen from throughout Anglo-Saxon England attended, but there was little or no royal involvement. We note that Theodore in formal writing styles himself "though unworthy, appointed bishop of the Church at Canterbury by the apostolic see," even though the term "archbishop" was already being used, as for example in II.3 and IV.1. For dating by indiction, see above at I.23. The list of bishops shows that their ecclesiastical designations are still primarily tribal rather than diocesan. The "said book of canons" referenced here may have been intended to indicate the canons of various early church councils, some of which had been translated into Latin in the sixth century, but recent scholarly study has shown that the particular wording of the chapters from the Hertford synod cannot be identified with any known texts of previous councils even though in some cases the thoughts are similar. The Hertford chapters or decrees are primarily disciplinary in character and regulatory of the clergy, reflecting the firm government heralded by Theodore's administration. Following public deliberation, Archbishop Theodore promulgates them in the first-person singular and thus by his own authority.

---

35. Derick W. Allen and A. Macdonald Allchin, "Primacy and Collegiality . . . ," *Journal of Ecumenical Studies* 2, no. 1 (Winter 1965): 63-80, at 68-69.

Chapter 1 of Hertford reaffirms the decision of the Synod of Whitby, which formally adopted the Roman calculation of Easter. Chapter 2 reveals the emerging nature of the territorial concept of a diocese; bishops are said to exercise authority over an area, not over a people or tribe. This was particularly important in a time when secular boundaries still could be easily moved and tribal areas shuffled by either war or treaty. Bishops are therefore not to invade the geographical territory of another bishop's diocese. (We note that the word translated here as "diocese" is the Latin *parrochia,* which at that time was still being used somewhat interchangeably with *diocesis.*) Chapter 3 exempts monasteries in a general way from episcopal jurisdiction. Chapter 4 addresses the perennial problem of wandering monks and affirms the concept of monastic vows as anchoring a monk to a particular religious house. Chapter 5 aims to stabilize clergy wandering without permission from their own bishop, under threat of excommunication for both the wanderer and the receiver. (In Anglo-Saxon translation, the word for "excommunication" here was rendered "biscopesdome," literally, "the bishop's doom," or legal judgment.) Chapter 6 limits the powers of clergy to the areas where they have the permission of the diocesan bishop to function in holy orders. The overall effect of chapters 4-6 is to limit the Celtic concept of "pilgrimage" and its ideal of "wandering for the sake of Christ." That older model with its emphasis on personal evangelism is thus somewhat subordinated to Roman obedience, as can be seen in Archbishop Theodore's deposing of Bishop Winfrith below at the beginning of IV.6. Chapter 7 stipulates yearly synods for each province, while reaffirming the ideal, which was suggested by canon 5 of the first ecumenical council of Nicaea in 325, that such synods should meet twice yearly. The place called Clofaeshoh, or Clovesho, convenient to London, has never been precisely identified.[36] Chapter 8 establishes episcopal rank by seniority of consecration (and not by importance or antiquity of the see). Chapter 9 reflects an unresolved dispute over basic strategy for missionary outreach and the method of pastoral care — in particular, whether the geographical boundaries of episcopal sees should be divided as they grow in size, or whether each diocese should sim-

---

36. On the location, now see Mechthild Gretsch, *Aelfric and the Cult of Saints in Late Anglo-Saxon England* (Cambridge: Cambridge University Press, 2005), p. 41.

ply be allowed to continue growing in numbers. Theodore is known to have favored some division into smaller dioceses, as is reported by Bede in the case of Bisi, bishop of the East Angles, here at the end of this account. (Bishop Wilfrid would soon move to oppose this principle, especially when he saw that his own vast diocese was liable to be subdivided; IV.13. See also the case of the Northumbrian churches in IV.12.) Chapter 10 went beyond the general canon law of the church, in prohibiting remarriage even of the innocent party. There seem to be no grounds for separation other than fornication, and no rights at all accorded to the wife.[37]

Overall the Synod of Hertford was significant in two ways. First, it introduced continental (indeed, Roman) forms of synodical government, familiar to Theodore, into the English Church. Second, it made the English Church a single ecclesiastical body capable of formal legislation under the archbishop of Canterbury, while politically England was still composed of several separate kingdoms.

Book IV.6

This may be a good place, in passing, to call attention to the balance of emphases in Bede's historical writing, as, on the one hand, he regularly enumerates the names and successions of bishops and abbots and abbesses and kings and bretwaldas (over-rulers, not a term used by Bede) and other leaders in what is sometimes called the "great men" theory of history (as we have already observed in his Preface), and, on the other hand, he also records instances of miracles and healing, of beams of heavenly light and visions of approaching death, that he has learned of but without passing judgment as to their historical veracity or whether they really happened. ("I think, however, that it would be far from fitting to pass over a miracle of healing," he remarks in IV.10.) Modern historians, by contrast, often seem to disregard the latter accounts entirely and to show interest in the

---

37. Good discussions of these canons are found in Godfrey, *Church in Anglo-Saxon England,* pp. 131-33, and Mayr-Harting, *The Coming of Christianity to England,* pp. 130-32, 139.

former only as a framework for writing histories that focus on "the little people" or "the common man," often as sociological illustrations of class struggles or other factors. Bede of course was writing in the early eighth century, and such "modern" concerns may not have occurred to him or he may not have had the materials available to write a history that began "from the bottom up."

Book IV.6-11

Barking was a double monastery for both women and men, of the sort that has been discussed earlier at III.8. The major source of Bede's information for this group of chapters was possibly a "Life of St. Aethelburh (Ethelburga), Abbess of Barking" that is now lost. In these chapters the title of "mother" or "mother of the community" or "mother of the congregation" *(mater congregationis)* is the term employed for women in positions of spiritual and administrative leadership, as it is also of St. Hilda in IV.23. We note in chapter 7 that the morning office of praise (presumably the services called Matins and Lauds) is being anticipated the night before, a not uncommon practice. We also note that the standard posture for prayer in this period is bowing or kneeling, in contrast to the standing posture that was common in the early church (cf. III.2).

The convent's interpretation of the boy Aesica's cry in IV.8 is a good example of a Christian interpretation of an otherwise neutral or ambiguous event. On the one hand, common sense indicates that a child in pain might call for someone close to him, especially in the hour of death. The eyes of faith, on the other hand, saw the boy's utterance as a true prophecy.

As we see in IV.9, many medieval Christians took 2 Corinthians 12:9 in a quite literal fashion. Here the nun Torhtgyth is said to be stricken by crippling disease "in order that her strength might be made perfect in weakness." The concept as presented here, and in a similar remark about Abbess Hilda at IV.23, is that the suffering itself is a purgative for sins. While the notion that mere suffering is spiritually beneficial no longer holds much sway in modern Christianity, the basic idea that one can nonetheless find God in suffering certainly remains a part of Christian spirituality.

Chapter 11 concludes with the burial of Sebbi, King of the East Saxons, in the (cathedral) church of St. Paul, London (cf. II.5).

Book IV.12

It is indicated from Chinese sources that the comet Bede uses to date events in this chapter was visible from August to October of 676, not 678. Whichever date is accepted, Bede is now writing of events within his own lifetime, near his own birth about the same year as the Synod of Hertford, 672/3 (IV.5). The division of the Northumbrian churches recorded here, apparently into two territorial dioceses each with a town at its center and a bishop at its head, does seem to be in keeping with the spirit of the ninth chapter of that same synod. Caedwalla becomes another English king who desires to end his days in Rome (cf. IV.5).

Book IV.13

The rather complicated life of Wilfrid is described in Bede mainly in this chapter and V.19. Chapter 13 here opens with a brief description of a small Celtic monastery in the vicinity of Bosham (near Chichester) led by the Irish monk Dicuill, whose brothers had not been able to convert any of their South Saxon neighbors to the faith. However, Bishop Wilfrid (of the Roman persuasion), by contrast, is successful both in preaching and converting, and, according to Bede, even teaches the people how to fish in order to obtain their food.

At the Synod of Whitby, as we have seen, Wilfrid was one of the principal advocates for adoption of Roman practices. His stridently pro-Roman position seems to have caused him some political difficulties in England. Although Wilfrid would frequently appeal to Rome in these disputes, often in person, he always returned to England to serve there. He pursued an appeal at Rome in 678, for example, in opposition to the proposed division of his diocese, returning in 680. Wilfrid exemplifies the close connections between preaching, baptizing, teaching, and living a life of humility and poverty. His ministry also seems to have taken on a strong social message in the miraculous catch of fish that he shared and in the more economically radical emancipation of the South Saxon slaves at their conversion to Christianity, which is noted by Bede at the end of this chapter. He died in 709 and his feast day is traditionally kept on October 12.

Book IV.14

The vision on the last day of the life of this little Saxon boy suffering in an epidemic shares some features in common with the end of the lives of Chad and others (cf. IV.3). The story of the appearance of Saints Peter and Paul in this boy's vision and the intercession of Saint Oswald who had been killed on the same very day that the boy died (August 5; cf. III.9-10) are skillfully interrelated by Bede here.

At the same time, Bede employs a remarkable variety of terminology to describe the Eucharist, utilizing in this one chapter no less than six different expressions for it: "mass has been celebrated" *(missae celebrentur)*, "let them celebrate masses" *(celebrent missas)*, "let all join in offering the heavenly sacrifices" *(communicent omnes sacrificiis caelestibus)*, "masses to be said" *(missas fieri)*, "the sacrifice and oblation of the Lord" *(dominicae oblationis)*, and "the celebration of masses" *(missarum celebratione)*. There are also subtle differences in the Penguin and Oxford translations, the Penguin always capitalizing the words Mass and Sacrifice and the Oxford never. The common medieval term for the Eucharist, *Missa* or "Mass," known as early as the time of St. Ambrose in the later fourth century (cf. I.26 above), was derived from the dismissal words used at the end of the service probably as early as the fifth century, *Ite missa est,* meaning "Go it is completed" or "Go you are dismissed" or "Go this is the dismissal." Of particular liturgical interest here is the inclusion of Holy Communion in the last rites for the boy. We note the reference to the boy's final communion as the *viaticum,* or "food to take on the journey," and that it includes both the Body and the Blood of Christ, as also in IV.3.

The cult of St. Oswald is described more fully in III.11-12.

Book IV.15-16

In these two chapters we read of the deeds of Caedwalla, king of the West Saxons (Gewisse), and especially of his destruction of the native population of the Isle of Wight. The device of taking an oath to God in return for God's assumed promise of some favor, not uncommon at this time, we have seen earlier in the vows that Bede records at II.9, III.13, and III.21. Caedwalla's conquest of Wight is an intriguing mixture of missionary effort and political expediency. On the one hand, Caedwalla sees the Christian God as the agent of his victory; on the other hand, Caedwalla still executes the local royalty after their conversion to the faith that he viewed as being affirmed by his victory. Astonishingly, the two young princes are baptized and then executed. Bede comments that the Isle of Wight did not receive a bishop until very late "because it was suffering under the affliction of alien rule." Although the concept of a geographic diocese was gaining ground in England, the older notion of tribal allegiance is seen here.

Book IV.17

Unlike Whitby, presided over by King Oswiu in 664, now with Hertford in 672/3 and Hatfield in 680 (or possibly 679) we have the first and second national synods or councils of the English Church convoked and presided over by its own leadership, Archbishop Theodore. The conventional site, which had been located as Hatfield in Hertfordshire, has now been challenged in favor of Hatfield near Doncaster in south Yorkshire. Whereas the canons of Hertford were primarily disciplinary in kind, Hatfield's decision was primarily one of Christological doctrine. Bede is clearly not a specialist in this area of controversy about Christ that intrigued the minds of many theologians of the early church, its background lying not in England but in the complex Christological disputes of the Eastern Churches.

Referenced at the beginning of this chapter, the monophysite "heresy of Eutyches," an archimandrite at Constantinople who held that God the Word after becoming flesh had only one nature *(mono-phusis)*, was condemned at the fourth ecumenical council of Chalcedon in 451. The contro-

versy had continued in the Christian East, however, and instead of "one nature" the emperor Heraclius in 638 had proposed that Christ had a "single
will" *(mono-thelema)*. Archbishop Theodore, who had been a Greek monk,
would have known of this monothelete doctrine, and here he is being en-
listed in the effort of Pope Agatho to condemn it and to ascertain that it has
not spread in England. Pope Agatho had sent Abbot John the precentor or
arch-cantor of the apostolic see to enquire of, and confirm, the orthodoxy
of the English Church on this matter, presumably in preparation for the
sixth ecumenical council of Constantinople in 680, which condemned both
monophysitism (Eutychianism) and monotheletism (also spelled, incor-
rectly, as monothelitism).

The opening of the synodal letter which makes up most of this chapter
indicates that there is now ecclesiastical unity in "the island of Britain," but
not yet political unity. Although Theodore at Hertford (IV.5) had styled
himself "Bishop of the See of Canterbury by the authority of the apostolic
see," here he calls himself "archbishop of the island of Britain and of the city
of Canterbury" but does not mention his appointment by the apostolic see,
as later archiepiscopal titles would come to do. The reference to "having the
most holy gospels before us" presumably refers to the ancient custom followed in the early ecumenical councils and other church synods, namely,
being a solemn exposition of a finely made book of the Gospels opened and
displayed in full view throughout the proceedings, as was still done at the
Second Vatican Council.

The word correctly translated as "creed" in the phrase "the creed of the
holy fathers," appearing in Bede's Latin as *symbolum,* was later translated as
"herebeacen" in the Anglo-Saxon version of Bede, a word which in Anglo-
Saxon could also mean "battle-standard."

After affirming the decisions of the first five universal (ecumenical, or
pertaining to the worldwide church) councils, Hatfield proceeds to condemn monotheletism by endorsing the first Lateran synod of 649 held at
Rome under Pope Martin I that had already condemned it. In the conclusion of the Hatfield synodal letter near the end of this chapter, we note that
Archbishop Theodore, although a Greek, also affirms the doctrine of the
double procession (of the Holy Spirit from the Father "and from the Son"),
or *filioque,* a matter which was, happily, not yet an issue of major dispute be-

tween East and West (although it would later become such). Here at Hatfield, therefore, the English Church affirms the first five ecumenical (or "general") councils, all that had been held thus far, even though English representatives did not participate in making all their decisions. It also aligns itself with the decision of the 649 Roman council, which was a local, not ecumenical, synod, held at Rome, against monotheletism, by endorsing the transcript that Abbot John (representing the Pope, as we see in the next chapter) has brought to it. It is also possible that the future Archbishop Theodore, then a Greek monk living in Rome, may have played a key role in those doctrinal proceedings against monotheletism in 649. The Synod of Hatfield, by all these actions, helps to prepare the way for the decision against monotheletism at the sixth ecumenical council at Constantinople in 680, whereby the two natures and two wills in Christ would soon be affirmed. (We also know from Book V.19 that Pope Agatho summoned a preparatory synod at Rome earlier in 680 to condemn monotheletism, which Wilfrid attended on behalf of the English Church.)

Book IV.18

Bede mentions the "Abbot Benedict" and indicates that this Benedict was already known to his readers, but this is not exactly true. Benedict Biscop, an English monk who in 669 had accompanied Archbishop Theodore to Canterbury and then served for a brief time as abbot of the monastery of Sts. Peter and Paul (later St. Augustine's) until the appointment of Hadrian, was subsequently the founder of the monastery of Monkwearmouth (674), which Bede had entered, and was obviously well known to Bede. (Monkwearmouth was also known as Wearmouth-Jarrow and was regarded as a single monastery with two locations under one abbot; cf. V.21.) Bede had not written of Benedict Biscop previously in this *History,* although he did in his *Lives of the Abbots.* (There are editions by J. Campbell and D. H. Farmer.) Abbot John, the arch-cantor of the apostolic see (i.e., precentor, or chief of the singers), had come from Rome with Abbot Benedict, bringing with him the decisions of the first Lateran synod of 649, held at Rome under Pope Martin I (cf. IV.17). He also seems to have introduced a second wave of Roman practice in church music, the first being under James the Deacon (cf. II.20).

Book IV.19

Queen Aethelthryth, also widely known as Etheldreda, enters the religious life and becomes the founding abbess of the double monastery of Ely (cf. III.8). Another, and abbreviated, form of her name is "Audrey." This account of her life and of the incorruption of her body after death gives evidence of the high esteem in which virginity was held at that time, an austerity that is matched by the reports of her woolen garments and her reluctance to bathe in hot water, her abstention from meals, and her intensity at morning prayers. The list of the major feasts for which Etheldreda made special observance does not include Christmas here, which may be an omission or may possibly reflect an early and Eastern custom of combining Christ's birth and his Epiphany (manifestation to the gentiles) in one feast. The last sentence of the second paragraph of the Penguin text seems to be mistranslated, and should better read with the Oxford edition "she was buried by her own command in a wooden coffin, in the ranks of the other nuns, as her turn came." The Penguin edition has Etheldreda dying in her coffin, which would seem somewhat strange, and the point is rather that she was buried next to the nun who had died last before her, rather than separately. The "small deserted fortress not far away which is called Grantchester in English" is a description of the town subsequently known as "Cambridge." St. Etheldreda's humble and holy life is confirmed, in Bede's view, by the events recorded here, and her feast day is traditionally kept on October 17.[38] Bede's remark at the end of chapter 19 seems accurate, that Ely "derives its name from the large number of eels which are caught in the marshes."

---

38. Further see Virginia Blanton, *Signs of Devotion: The Cult of St. Aethelthryth in Medieval England, 695-1615* (University Park, Penn.: Pennsylvania State University Press, 2007).

Book IV.20

This acrostic poem of elegiac metre in praise of virginity and of Aethelthryth or Etheldreda, purportedly composed by Bede himself and recalling six virgin martyrs of the early church by name, was not accompanied by its introductory paragraph in the earlier Penguin versions as it is now and as also in the Oxford text. Bede's reference to the Roman poet Virgil (Maro) is intended to recall the first lines of his *Aeneid*, "I sing of arms and the man" (in Latin, *Arma virumque cano)*. In the Penguin and Oxford translations of Bede today, as well as in the Oxford Latin text edited by Colgrave and Mynors, every line of the acrostic begins, in abecedarian structure, with a letter of the alphabet in succession (except J and W, which have no place in the Latin alphabet), followed by four final lines whose beginning letters spell AMEN. The abbreviations X, XT, or XRIST, are used for "Christ."

Book IV.21

Here we see the intervention of Archbishop Theodore, "beloved of God" *(Theodorus Deo dilectus antistes),* to prevent a further decay of a bad political situation. The compensation arranged here, known as *wergild,* was a large payment by the offending party to the family of the one who had been killed, to avoid retaliation by bloodshed. Generally, the church stood in favor of this peaceful method of compensation rather than the alternative of blood-feud.

Book IV.22

The origins of the custom of offering the Eucharist for the repose of the soul of a departed Christian go back far into the depths of Christian antiquity, and already Gregory the Great c. 593 in his *Dialogues* (cf. IV.57) had taught that the Eucharist could properly be offered for that purpose. Bede's variety of terms used to describe the offering of the Eucharist has already been explored above in the comments at IV.14. Later, such Masses celebrated with particular intention for the faithful departed came to be known as "Requiem Masses" from the first word of the Introit or opening words said at the beginning of such Masses, although Bede is writing too early in the Middle Ages to use terminology such as this, just as he is writing too early to comment upon the buying or selling of such Masses (as was later done). But there is the clear implication here that the pains of the afterlife that await Imma (a *thegn,* or courtier, sometimes spelled "thane," who has been captured and bound by a *gesith,* or nobleman) can be alleviated by the Masses and prayers offered here and now by his brother Tunna who is a priest. And the fact that Tunna is offering these Masses "for the absolution of his [brother's] soul" *(pro absolutione animae eius)* indicates that "absolution," or forgiveness of sin, and not just "repose," is the result that is hoped for and the efficacy expected (expressed at the end of the chapter in terms of "deliverance" and "everlasting redemption"). The term "purgatory" is not used, however, and there is no talk here of an intermediate state. What interests Bede most of all, either actually or symbolically, is the loosening of Imma's chains that happens frequently at the time of Terce (*a tercia hora,* "about nine in the morning," i.e., the third hour of sun-filled day) (cf. III.5), the very time that Tunna was usually celebrating Mass for Imma, as well as the implication that others might also benefit from a similar devotion of such celebrations of the Eucharist.

Book IV.23

Hilda, foundress and abbess of Whitby (Streaneshalch, North Yorkshire), is perhaps the most widely known female saint of early England. At the Whitby synod itself she had sided with the Celtic party, but loyally accepted the decision for the Roman dating of Easter. The monastic rule at Whitby seems to have been developed by Hilda personally (her name is translated "Hild" in the Oxford text). Bede approvingly describes this rule as being "after the example of the primitive church," with neither rich nor needy, with all things held in common, and no personal property. This double monastery at Whitby was extraordinarily prolific in its preparation of men for ordination (described in the Latin text as *ecclesiasticum gradum, hoc est altaris officium*) and in its nurture of future bishops, all under the direction of Hilda. The terminology of "mother" as well as the notion of illness being a purgative have also been noted in Bede's account of Ethelburga in IV.9.

Bede's rich description of Hilda's deathbed provides early evidence of a number of attendant customs such as the *viaticum* (cf. IV.14) and the passing bell. Her feast day is generally celebrated on November 17 or 18. The Oxford translation describes her as having been "ordained" by Bishop Aidan, the Latin reading *consecrante Aidano episcopo,* but this early and non-technical terminology in Bede is not intended to indicate conferral of Holy Orders and the Penguin's "with the blessing of Bishop Aidan" is less literal but more accurate.

Book IV.24

As it is told here by Bede, its only source, the story of Caedmon (fl. 658-680) recounts the latter part of the life of the earliest English Christian poet known by name.[39] Caedmon's hymn as paraphrased by Bede here, the only certain piece of his work to survive, has been described as the earliest recorded poem in the English language. Recalling the beginning of Genesis and singing the biblical accounts of creation in this way, Caedmon the cowherd delights his hearers with his beautiful songs and is received into the community of Whitby by the abbess. Having a premonition of his own death, he calls for the Eucharist (*viaticum,* reserved in the infirmary for the communion of the sick), arranges his dispositions to be in love and charity with all, makes the sign of the cross, and dies. Bede tells us almost all we know of him. His feast is kept on the eleventh of February in some places.

It is interesting to note, in this chapter as well as throughout, that for Bede the "Eucharist" is generally an object and not an action, the Eucharistic act of worship itself being generally called the "Mass" and, by contrast, "the Eucharist" being the sacramental object or the sacred food of communion, whereas today both Eucharist and Mass are used almost interchangeably to describe the same action of the worship. The "Mass," however, is used today only to describe the action and not the object, whereas the "Eucharist" can be either.

39. Cf. Godfrey, *Church in Anglo-Saxon England,* p. 188, and Deanesly, *The Pre-Conquest Church,* pp. 168-69. Many studies of Caedmon exist, as well as online recordings at various websites.

Book IV.25

At the double monastery of Coldingham, located in Berwickshire, Scotland (forty-five miles from Edinburgh and a short bus ride from Berwick-on-Tweed), the discipline had become decidedly lax and the abbess Aebbe (Ebba, "the mother of the congregation," Bede calls her) seems surprisingly unawares. The Irish monk Adamnan, having made private confession of his sins there and receiving an appropriate penance, has a vision that the entire monastery will be destroyed by fire. Bede therefore takes the opportunity, not so subtly, to warn his readers that unless they atone for their sins by good works their bad deeds may be punished and God's retribution may come.

The sacramental confession made by Adamnan in the Coldingham monastery is characteristic of the early medieval period in the history of sacramental reconciliation, in process of development by Celtic and Anglo-Saxon monks at this time, although Bede does not tell us what penitential book is being followed. By now, the confession has become private and secret (one-to-one, and the offenses not a matter of public knowledge), for a plurality of minor sins as well as major ones (not just for apostasy, adultery, or murder), repeatable, regulated by priests but not by bishops, and with a penance graded to fit the offense ("A severe wound calls for an even more severe remedy"), but the process still retains one feature of the earlier patristic custom in that absolution/reconciliation will not be pronounced until after the penance is performed. (Later in the medieval period, the final sequence will be reversed and absolution will be given first, as is still the case today, upon promise of satisfaction, restitution, or penance to be performed later.) Adamnan, however, having promised to perform his penance, is now left in uncertainty when the priest leaves for Ireland and dies there, and Adamnan must remain unsure how or when he will ever receive absolution once his penance is done. Bede summarizes Adamnan's only option: "He ever afterwards, in accordance with his promise, maintained this same standard of austerity; and though he had begun this way of life in the fear of God and in penitence for his guilt, he now continued it unweariedly for the love of God and because he delighted in its rewards." (This Adamnan, we should note, is not the person of the same name that we shall encounter in Book V.15.)

Book IV.26

Like the previous chapter, this one also reveals Bede's understanding about divine retribution in history. King Ecgfrith seems bent on the expansion of his territory even against the opinions of his religious advisors. His first efforts, against the Irish, are successful, but his campaign against the Picts the next year ends in his demise. Unlike the Irish who were adopting English ecclesiastical customs in a piecemeal fashion, the Picts, who occupied the far northern reaches of modern Scotland, were not under even nominal English control and hence, for Bede, the loss to them was particularly appalling.

Book IV.27

King Ecgfrith in 685 had caused Cuthbert to be consecrated *(fecerat ordinari)* as bishop of Lindisfarne. Along with Augustine, Aidan, and Chad, Cuthbert is one of Bede's model bishops. Much of the material about Cuthbert that we read in IV.27-32 is also found (along with some stories of miracles) in Bede's *Life of Cuthbert*. Research on Cuthbert was the occasion for Bede's one known visit to Lindisfarne. Colgrave and Mynors remark, at this point in their original edition of the Oxford text: "It may well have been that to Bede Cuthbert symbolized the union of the Celtic and Roman Churches, the establishment of good relations with Rome again while all that was best of the Irish tradition remained."[40] And Cuthbert exemplifies all that Bede admires in a bishop. He preaches the Word, teaches, travels on foot, lives in poverty, practices humility, and follows the fathers of the primitive church. Cuthbert's wandering evangelism is technically not the sort that was forbidden at the Synod of Hertford because of his attachment to a particular place to which he returned (see above, IV.5).

One of the most famous and most beautiful illuminated texts of the Gospels comes from Lindisfarne from the late seventh or early eighth century, just a few decades after the time of Oswald and Aidan but even closer to the time of Cuthbert. Three centuries later this illuminated manuscript

40. Bertram Colgrave and R. A. B. Mynors, eds., *Bede's Ecclesiastical History of the English People* (Oxford: Clarendon, 1998; 1st edition 1969), p. xxxiv.

would become the first complete version of the Gospels in English when Aldred converted it into a parallel text by adding a word-for-word Old English (Anglo-Saxon) interlinear translation between the lines of the Latin.[41]

Book IV.28

Cuthbert's monastic seclusion described in the first half of this chapter was typical of Celtic monks. Whenever a Celtic religious community or person relocated, it seems that the custom was first to drive out the evil spirits with prayer and then to look to the material sustenance that would be needed for living. The island of basalt rock to which Cuthbert (and earlier Aidan) would retreat for prayer and solitude, very near on the mainland side of Lindisfarne and called "Hobthrush," can still be easily reached today. Cuthbert's miraculous spring or well there carries echoes of the story in the account of Alban's martyrdom in Book I.7 and had its biblical prototype in Exodus 17.

There was apparently another church synod held under Archbishop Theodore, at Twyford ("Adtuifyrdi") in Northumbria, in the autumn of 684, about which very little is known. At this synod, Bede tells us, Cuthbert was "elected" bishop of Lindisfarne, although Bede has already told us at the beginning of chapter 27 that King Ecgfrith had caused Cuthbert to be consecrated *(fecerat ordinari)* to the same see. Although the account is complicated by some possible confusion on Bede's part, there seems to have been a friendly reshuffling of bishops that resulted with Eata in the see of Hexham and Cuthbert in Lindisfarne, which Cuthbert preferred. "Only after winter," Bede tells us, Cuthbert was finally consecrated by Theodore, assisted by six other bishops, at York at the festival of Easter in the year 685.

At the end of this chapter, Bede tells us that when Cuthbert "offered up the saving Victim as a sacrifice to God" (i.e., celebrated the Mass), he would shed tears *(lacrimae)* "which sprang from the depths of his heart," a not uncommon phenomenon in medieval spirituality that is recorded, for example, of St. Thomas Becket at some of his celebrations of Mass in the late twelfth century. It is sometimes called "compunction."

41. The definitive study is now *The Lindisfarne Gospels: Society, Spirituality and the Scribe* by Michelle P. Brown (London: British Library, 2003).

Book IV.29

Cuthbert, like so many saints, has a premonition of his own death (cf. Caedmon in IV.24). His ongoing humility as a bishop is evidenced by his willingness to seek spiritual advice from the hermit, Herbert, and they both die in the hermitage on Farne Island in the same year 687 on the same day, March 20, which is traditionally kept as the feast of St. Cuthbert. Cuthbert had reached the age of fifty-three. In Bede's account, as elsewhere with other persons at death, we read of the angels bearing the souls of the departed upwards to heaven (examples: IV.3, IV.23), a belief that will eventually find expression in the commendatory anthem concluding the liturgical rite for funerals: "Into paradise may the angels lead thee; and at thy coming may the martyrs receive thee, and bring thee into the holy city Jerusalem."

Book IV.30

Cuthbert's body, like those of so many saints, is later found to be incorrupt. (For other examples, see III.8, above.) The reason given for this discovery was the desire of the monks to elevate Cuthbert's remains to a place of greater honor and accessibility. Moving Cuthbert's body also seems to have provided room for his successor Bishop Eadberht to be buried at the same place. This was not to be the last time Cuthbert's body was disturbed or his coffin opened, being moved under Viking threats in the ninth century and eventually coming to Durham in the year 995. The magnificent shrine of St. Cuthbert at Durham Cathedral was desecrated and destroyed by the reformation in 1539-1540, but his body was later reburied in the Chapel of the Nine Altars there on the site now marked by a slab and the single word *Cuthbertus*. His wooden coffin was opened at Durham in 1104, 1827, and 1899.[42] Among the findings was a fine pectoral cross of gold, 6.4 cm. across in width, set with red garnet stones (the workmanship possibly dated to the period 640-670, in which case he may have worn it even as a priest, as was occasionally done by priests at that time, and be-

42. See further, C. F. Battiscombe, ed., *The Relics of St. Cuthbert,* and G. Bonner, D. Rollason, and G. Stancliffe, eds., *St. Cuthbert, His Cult and His Community to AD 1200* (Woodbridge: Boydell Press, 1989).

Pectoral Cross of St. Cuthbert, preserved in the crypt of Durham Cathedral. Cuthbert's coffin was opened at Durham in 1104, 1827, and 1899. See C. F. Battiscombe, ed., *The Relics of St. Cuthbert*. Among the findings was a fine pectoral cross of gold, 6.4 cm. across, set with red garnet stones. The workmanship may date to 640-670, in which case Cuthbert may have worn it even as a priest, as was occasionally done by priests at that time, and before he served as bishop of Lindisfarne, 685-687. *(© Jarrold Publishing and Durham Cathedral, reproduced by kind permission of the publisher.)*

fore he served as bishop of Lindisfarne 685-687). Also found were the head of King Oswald, the bones of St. Aidan, a small portable altar, a comb, a maniple, and other objects. The coffin and some of these are now exhibited in a hall within the crypt of Durham Cathedral. The Stonyhurst pocket gospel of John, which reveals the earliest binding of a manuscript to survive in Western Europe, has been on deposit in the British Library since the 1970s.

Book IV.31-32

The healing of Baduthegn provides a first-hand account of a miracle. Up to this point, Bede has always presented his sources for miracles as being trustworthy but second-hand. Here, in this case, Baduthegn is alive, and presumably would have been willing to corroborate the account of his healing. As for the specific ailment from which Baduthegn suffered, Bede gives a pretty clear description of what appears to be a sudden stroke, including a noteworthy awareness that its origin was located in the brain and not in the parts of the body affected by paralysis.

Another miraculous healing, this one resulting from Cuthbert's relics and not merely from his heavenly intercessions, is also told from a first-hand account in IV.32. The emphasis on the man's faith as operating in concert with the power of the relic itself is consonant with other healings in Bede, although this miracle is presented as occurring over an extended period of time rather than instantly as is usually the case.

Book V.1

The contents of Book V are the most miscellaneous of the five books in Bede's *History,* as he continues and gathers up his story of the English Church from the time of St. John of Beverley down to the year 731. Bede died in 735, possibly before he had time for a final arrangement of the various miracles, pilgrimages, and successions of bishops contained in Book V, and he closes this book with a chronological summary followed by a synopsis of his own life and works.

Chapter 1 here records a miracle by Cuthbert's successor, Ethelwald ("Oethelwald"), who, we note, assumes a kneeling posture for prayer. The miracle of calming the sea has its precedents both in Scripture and in the stories of early English saints. The first-person narrative style in this chapter and other places in Book V marks something of a departure from Bede's earlier style that we have observed. This is likely due to the simple fact that Bede is now dealing with first-person accounts rather than historical documents or second-hand oral accounts.

Book V.2-3

The church's ministry of healing in this period of history is performed at least partly through miracles, exemplified in these two chapters in the accounts Bede tells of St. John of Beverley, bishop of Hexham, who had ordained him. Bishop John teaches the alphabet and heals a boy's speech impediment in chapter 2, using the sign of the cross which was central to much early Christian piety. As with many of the miracles Bede records, a naturalistic explanation of the miracle is also possible, and one commentator, for example, has suggested that the healing of this boy is perhaps an early instance of the art of speech therapy, rather than a "miracle" as such.

In the subsequent chapter Bede gives his own eye-witness account of a nun whose swollen arm has been made worse by the process of blood-letting, a common but dubious medical practice at that time, and who is healed by the prayer of John of Beverley. Perhaps more interesting than the healing is the fact that the abbess had plans to appoint the nun, her own daughter, as abbess in her place. The fact that Bede sees no need to comment on this indication of hereditary succession is itself a subtle commentary on the practice, and the same can be said of the heirs of Swidberht at Kaiserswerth in V.11.

Book V.4-6

In addition to the early foundations of the cathedral churches, the minster churches, and the monastic churches, there are now oratory churches being founded and endowed by lay nobility in this period on their private estates for prayer and the use of family and household servants, and these will become the parish churches of the future. In these two chapters we get a good picture of how this is happening, as the nobles *(gesiths)* Puch and Addi proceed to found and endow such churches on their country manor-houses or estates and then present them to the bishop for dedication or consecration. These private proprietary churches, or "churches of the second foundation," will become known to later historians by the German term of *eigenkirchen.*[43] The church at Escomb (co. Durham) is conjectured to be a surviving example of a church founded in this way. The private ownership of thousands of these newer churches will become a problem by the time of the investiture contest in the eleventh and twelfth centuries, as the laity struggled to retain control of the churches that their ancestors endowed but whose revenues they often diverted to secular purpose and to which they sought to appoint clergy from their own families. The services used for consecrating such churches, which included the blessing of holy water as we see here, would soon begin to take fixed liturgical forms, although the use of the same water for healing, drinking, and washing did not perdure.

In chapters 5 and 6 Bede tells other stories of healing accomplished in response to the prayers of St. John of Beverley, including the curious story of the bishop's regularization of an imperfect baptism. This was probably not a case of rebaptism, as the Latin text says nothing about "validity," a term used only in the Penguin translation, whereas the Latin reads *non perfecte,* which is literally rendered in the text of the Oxford translation as "not perfectly." At a minimum, the bishop thought it had been inadequate. John of Beverley held the see of York from 705 until his death in 721, and Bede presents his miracles as the continuation of God's action in the history of the English Church.[44]

---

43. There is a good discussion in Godfrey, *Church in Anglo-Saxon England,* chapter 19.

44. Further see Susan E. Wilson, *The Life and After-Life of St. John of Beverly: The Evolution of the Cult of an Anglo-Saxon Saint* (London: Ashgate, 2006).

Book V.7

Caedwalla, king of the West Saxons, whom we last saw in an unfavorable light at IV.15-16, becomes another English king to make pilgrimage to Rome in this period (cf. IV.5), his purpose being to seek baptism at the shrine of the Prince of the Apostles. He is baptized there on the Saturday before Easter Sunday, the most traditional time in the liturgical year for that sacrament to be administered because it linked the symbolic dying and rising with Christ in the waters of baptism to Christ's own death on Good Friday and resurrection on Easter. Bede tells us that the king hoped to die shortly after his baptism, a not uncommon wish for Christians at that time who took literally the creedal belief in only "one baptism for the remission of sins," a belief that they would presumably profess at the very time of their own baptism. It was a common practice in this period to defer baptism until near the time of death in an effort to prevent the commission of further sins, which were believed as possibly unforgivable since they had occurred after baptism. Literally, people wanted to die while forgiven and before they might sin again. Apparently King Caedwalla got his wish, for he died while still wearing the white robes that were worn after baptism within the octave of Easter and before the following Sunday, traditionally called *Dominica in albis deponendis,* or "the Sunday when the white robes are laid aside." It is not clear whether the Pope himself performed this baptism, but Bede tells us that Pope Sergius did give Caedwalla a new baptismal name, that of Peter himself, and apparently authorized his burial in the church of St. Peter, to which the epitaph attests. Caedwalla's successor, Ine, also makes a pilgrimage to Rome, as do several other English people of both high and low estate (cf. IV.5, 12; V.9, 19).[45]

---

45. Further on such English pilgrimages to Rome at this time, see Allen and Allchin, "Primacy and Collegiality"; W. J. Moore, *The Saxon Pilgrims to Rome and the Schola Saxonum* (Freiburg, 1937); and W. Levison, *England and the Continent in the Eighth Century* (Oxford: Clarendon, 1946), pp. 36-44.

Book V.8

At the ripe age of eighty-eight, Archbishop Theodore of Tarsus dies on 19 September 690, on which day he is now generally commemorated in liturgical calendars. Not surprisingly, Bede gives high praise to Theodore's magnificent achievement in leading, organizing, and unifying the English Church, which he had served as archbishop of Canterbury for twenty-two years. Under him, at the end of the seventh century, Canterbury had also become a major seat of learning where both Greek and Latin were seriously taught, and where biblical commentaries on the Pentateuch and the Gospels were being written — commentaries of a genre that, uniquely for their era and rather unlike those of Bede himself, eschewed allegorical interpretation and mainly followed the Antiochene, or literal/historical, method of Scriptural exegesis. Theodore had already been consecrated archbishop before Bede was born and he died the year before Bede was made deacon, and for Bede Archbishop Theodore (together with Abbot Hadrian) had represented the primary contacts he had with the outside world and the wider church. A great theologian, linguist, canonist, and biblical scholar, Theodore was also immensely successful in bringing the English Church into line with Roman practice, at the same time making whatever adaptations he thought necessary. "A great high priest," the epitaph calls him in the Oxford translation ("a prince of pontiffs" in the Penguin), and Bede's description of Theodore reaches its climax when Bede declares that "the English Churches made more spiritual progress while he was archbishop than ever before." A splendid and scholarly volume of essays on his life and influence has been published, as well as the texts and an analysis of the surviving biblical commentaries produced at Canterbury under his tutelage and that of his colleague Hadrian.[46]

---

46. Michael Lapidge, ed., *Archbishop Theodore: Commemorative Studies on His Life and Influence* (Cambridge Studies in Anglo-Saxon England 11; Cambridge University Press, 1995); Bernhard Bischoff and Michael Lapidge, eds., *Biblical Commentaries from the Canterbury School of Theodore and Hadrian,* Cambridge Studies in Anglo-Saxon England 10 (Cambridge: Cambridge University Press, 1994).

Book V.9

Church Latin was a very fluid language, especially at this time, and here we have someone — Egbert — who in the opening line of this chapter is called *sacerdos* by Bede, a word translated as "priest" in the Oxford edition but "bishop" in the Penguin edition, whereas later on in this same chapter Bede also calls Boisil a *sacerdos,* which both editions translate as "priest." In Bede's Latin a *sacerdos* can be a priest or a bishop, somewhat interchangeably, whereas the word "priest" can also translate the Latin *presbyter* in Bede, but generally Bede does not use the term *presbyter* when he intends to indicate someone who is a bishop. This ambivalence of meaning for *sacerdos,* in Egbert's case, is admitted by the editors of the Oxford critical text at III.4, where they translate it as "priest"; for another instance, but not involving Egbert, see also III.21, above. The fluidity of the Latin, in this way, serves to increase the ambiguity of the English! We have earlier encountered Egbert at III.27, IV.3, and IV.26, and we shall see him again at V.22.

Bede's use of the Latin language is also capable of deeper meanings that can enrich us, as we see in the same sentence here with the English phrase "living a life of exile," which translates the Latin word *peregrinus* (used to describe Egbert) in both the Penguin and Oxford editions but which can just as accurately be translated "pilgrim." The point for Bede is that pilgrims of this sort, like Egbert, are exiles on the way to their "heavenly home" because they have no permanent dwelling on this earth. *Peregrinus* in this sense was a word used in the Christian Latin of late antiquity as well as in the early Middle Ages somewhat interchangeably with the word *paroikos,* borrowed from the New Testament Greek of 1 Peter 2:11 to indicate a temporary resident of earth on the way to heaven, a citizen "away from" one's native home (*para* in Greek meaning "away from" and *oikia* in Greek meaning "home") and thus one who in this life has "no abiding city" (Hebrews 13:14). As things happen, Egbert's proposed pilgrimage to Rome is canceled by a heavenly message, and soon thereafter the visions that Egbert ignores are confirmed in their divine origin by a storm that scuttles the ship that Egbert had intended to use. The reference later in this chapter to Wihtberht's living a life of exile draws on the same imagery of the Christian as *peregrinus* or *paroikos* or "pilgrim," a temporary sojourner who is merely traveling through this world. Such imagery was the basic and original meaning of the word "parishioner," before the terminology moved from early Christian times to take on more of a geographical meaning as the church's self-understanding became more landed and territorial when it began to enter the feudal system of the early Middle Ages in the centuries soon after Bede. For the same theme, also see V.21.

Book V.10

With the encouragement of Egbert, this group of itinerant preachers and missionaries pays a call upon the famous Frankish ruler Pippin (Pepin) II, under whose leadership conversions to Christianity seem more probable, as seen in the story of the Anglo-Saxon missionary priests and brothers known as the Hewalds (Ewalds). Bede's version of their martyrdom is also notable for its reference to the offering of daily Mass ("daily offering up the sacrifice of the saving Victim to God") upon a portable altar, which was likely a small, square or oblong table specifically consecrated for that purpose and probably similar to the one found in the coffin of St. Cuthbert (IV.30). We note that Bede's word for "priest" in this chapter is *presbyter,* not *sacerdos.* The relics of the Hewalds were still said to be seen in the church of St. Cunibert on the banks of the Rhine near Cologne Cathedral in modern times.

Book V.11

There is some chronological overlap in Bede's accounts of Willibrord, whom earlier in III.13 we already saw as "archbishop of the Frisians" and a former student of Wilfrid. Willibrord's first trip to Rome (693), at the beginning of this chapter, is to gain the blessing of Pope Sergius for the nascent mission to the Frisians and to obtain relics of saints which by this time in history are increasingly viewed as necessary contents that must be obtained for the altar of the patron saint of every new church being founded. Now in V.11 we finally read of Willibrord's consecration as archbishop by the Pope, apparently on his second trip to Rome (695) and with the endorsement of Pippin.[47] While Willibrord is understood as being the proto-evangelist to the Frisians and the first bishop of the see of Utrecht, Bede in this context seems to regard Swithberht as their first bishop. Bede in this chapter clearly designates episcopacy by his use of the Latin words *episcopatus* and *antistites*.

St. Willibrord died in 739 at the monastery of Echternach in Luxemburg which he had founded, and his feast day is generally observed on 7 November. The Society of St. Willibrord, founded in the early twentieth century, exists for the sake of friendship and closer relations between Anglicans and the "Old Catholic" churches in these lands who split from the papacy in 1870 over objection to the doctrine of papal infallibility and other matters.

Book V.12-14

These chapters are given over to visions of the other world and experiences of life after death. In the opening lines of chapter 12 Bede indicates the two reasons why he thinks these miracles are important: because they "occurred in Britain," and because they have the power "to arouse the living from spiritual death." At the end of chapter 12 we are told that the name of the man who returned from death to tell all these experiences is "Dryhthelm," whom Bede has preferred to remain anonymous until the very end of the story, omitting the name at the first, possibly for dramatic effect. Modern readers of Bede, observing for example in Dryhthelm's account the widespread medieval belief that hell was both extremely hot and extremely cold, will be tempted to seek or imagine parallels with Dante's *Divine Comedy* that was written several centuries later, but in Bede there is not yet the formal structure or theological rationale of life after death that would be developed by

---

47. For the so-called "Calendar of St. Willibrord," its contents and dating around this time, see Catherine Cubitt, pp. 439-43 of Alan Thacker and Richard Sharpe, eds., *Local Saints and Local Churches in the Early Medieval West* (Oxford: Oxford University Press, 2002).

the time of the high Middle Ages. The closest parallel with that system is Bede's assertion here that the departed are assisted by the prayers, alms, and fasting of the living and the Masses they offer (cf. IV.22).

Chapters 13 and 14 carry the obvious and urgent message that repentance should be made, and the *viaticum* received, before reaching one's deathbed (cf. IV.14, 23, 24).

Book V.15

Here Bede records the further spread and increasing acceptance of the Roman dating of Easter throughout formerly Celtic areas, as well as the spread of other Roman practices, under the leadership of Adamnan, abbot of Iona 679-704. Bede tells us that Adamnan "altered his opinion," having been advised "that he, in company with a very small band of followers, living in the remotest corner of the world, should not presume to go against the universal custom of the church." No doubt with some regret, however, Bede adds that Adamnan failed to persuade his own monastery of Iona, located off the extreme northwestern coast of modern Scotland, to accept the Roman practice. Adamnan's name is also spelled "Adomnan," and he wrote a *Life of St. Columba* which Bede does not know, but he is not the same "Adamnan" whom we encountered at Coldingham in IV.25.

Book V.15-17

Adamnan also wrote a work entitled *De Locis Sanctis,* a description of the Holy Land based upon information he had received from Arculf, a bishop from Gaul who had traveled there, and Bede in V.15-17 paraphrases from Adamnan's work that draws upon the description thereof written by Arculf around the year 680. His observations reflect Jerusalem as it would have appeared under the period of Islamic domination that began with the Muslim caliph Omar in 638 and continued for centuries thereafter. Here we read important descriptions of Bethlehem and its grotto, the Church of the Nativity, Constantine's Church of the Holy Sepulchre in Jerusalem ("called the Martyrium"), the Church of Golgotha and its enormous silver cross, the crypt where the remains of the True Cross were found and where "the sacrifice is offered for the honored dead," the Anastasis or Church of the Resurrection, and the Tomb itself. Also we note the Church of the Ascension on the Mount of Olives, the tombs of the patriarchs at Hebron (Abraham, Isaac, and Jacob), the oak of Mamre, and still other holy places.

Always the historian, Bede takes care to confront his readers with the historical roots of the worldwide church and also to alert his readers at the end of V.17 to his sources and the liberty he has taken with them.[48]

Book V.18

Apparently in accord with chapter 9 of the Synod of Hertford (IV.5, IV.12) and the principles of the late Archbishop Theodore, the division of the see of Wessex into smaller dioceses upon the death of Bishop Haedde is probably an indication of the growth of Christianity in this area. This supposition receives further support from Aldhelm's account of the cult of Haedde and miracles attributed to his relics. Aldhelm (d. 709), one of the two men appointed bishop in the new smaller dioceses cut out of Wessex, and formerly abbot of Malmesbury, was also a great literary figure of the seventh century. As the spread of Christianity is often marked by an increase in the numbers of bishops and dioceses, the note at the very end of this chapter about the South Saxon bishopric having fallen into abeyance is likely to in-

---

48. Although he had never been there, Bede's descriptions of Jerusalem and the Holy Land do ring true, both with the earliest accounts and with modern ones. For the former, see John Wilkinson, ed., *Egeria's Travels to the Holy Land,* revised edition (Jerusalem: Ariel Publishing, 1981); George Gingras, ed., *Egeria: Diary of a Pilgrimage,* Ancient Christian Writers 39 (Westminster, Md.: Newman Press, 1970); and for an interesting comparison of both Adamnan's writing and Bede's on the same subject see P. Geyer in *Itinere Hierosolymitana* (CSEL, 1898): 221-324. For modern descriptions of the Holy Places, especially of the most important one, see Martin Biddle, *The Tomb of Christ* (Stroud: Sutton Publishing, 1999), and J. Robert Wright, *The Holy Sepulchre: The Church of the Resurrection, An Ecumenical Guide* (Jerusalem: Ecumenical Theological Research Fraternity in Israel, 1998).

dicate either a failed missionary bishopric or a resurgence of earlier pagan religion. For miracles of healing related to sacred earth mixed in water, see III.13 and IV.3.

Book V.19

Still other English royalty make pilgrimage to Rome and enter religious houses there (cf. IV.5, 12; V.7, 9). Bede has already given us pictures of Wilfrid in III.28 and IV.13 and 19, and now Bede offers a retrospective survey. We note that Bede's narrative of the life of Wilfrid leaves out Wilfrid's love of wealth and rather "secular" style of life, which had been included in the contemporary biography of Wilfrid by Eddius.[49] Bede almost certainly had Eddius's biography of Wilfrid at hand when he was writing his *History,* and Bede's reason for omission of the less flattering features of Wilfrid's life is not hard to deduce. Wilfrid, as Bede himself tells us, was an early and ardent supporter of "Catholic," or Roman, usages in Northumbria, and it seems likely that Bede wanted to paint the best possible picture of him.

Wilfrid protested deprivation from his see of Northumbria by Theodore of Tarsus (see IV.5, 12, and 13), and his appeal to Pope Agatho, 678-680, over this matter is sustained there. While at Rome in 680 Wilfrid also represents the English Church at the synod called by Pope Agatho to condemn monotheletism in preparation for the sixth ecumenical council (cf. IV.17), presenting himself as a true English churchman doing what he can to help the church even though he has some personal complaint against the church's actions. Later Wilfrid was again deprived of the see of York, and he appeals a second time to Rome, this time before Pope John VI in 703, and it too is sustained. In these appeals to the papacy, the earliest perhaps being that over the vacancy of the see of Canterbury in the years 664-668 (III.29-30), it becomes clear that the English Church is now very much a part of the universal church whose (western) center is at Rome. English appeals to

49. There are modern versions of this work by Eddius, edited by J. F. Webb in the Penguin *Lives of the Saints,* by D. H. Farmer in *The Age of Bede,* and by C. Albertson in *Anglo-Saxon Saints and Heroes.*

Rome will become a problem particularly in the later Middle Ages, and at the reformation the English crown will absolutely forbid them. Here, nothing is said about Wilfrid's need to obtain royal permission before making such appeal.

In the middle of this chapter, the Oxford translation seems entirely accurate (and realistic) in stating that Wilfrid "studied" each of the Gospels in turn, thus avoiding the impression that he actually "memorized" them, whereas the Penguin translation records that Wilfrid "mastered each of the Gospels in turn" (an earlier Penguin edition even said that Wilfrid *learned* each of the Gospels in turn). Bede's original Latin reads *didicit.*

Book V.20

Wilfrid's death took place in 709. Here in V.20, his successor as bishop of Hexham, Acca, gathers up relics of the apostles and martyrs and builds altars for their veneration. In accord with the piety of the era, relics of the saints in this period are now frequently being gathered from their burial places and placed upon or enclosed within altars for veneration and intercession, thereby "establishing various chapels for this purpose within the walls of the church," which Bede obviously considers to be an appropriate development.

Kent remains the center of Roman influence in liturgical music as seen in the recruitment of a specialist named Maban, "instructed in methods of singing by the successors of the disciples of St. Gregory in Kent" (cf. II.20; IV.2).

Book V.21

It has been suggested that Bede himself had a considerable hand in composing this letter from Abbot Ceolfrith to Nechtan king of the Picts, and it is certainly the longest document that Bede includes in his *History.* This is Nechtan IV, who ascended the Pictish throne in 706. Ceolfrith is the abbot of Bede's own monastery, that of Wearmouth-Jarrow, also known as Monkwearmouth (cf. IV.18), founded by Benedict Biscop in 674 and 680

Exterior of St. Paul's Monastery Church at Jarrow, established over the years 680-685 under Ceolfrid, prior of Monkwearmouth, who became first abbot of Jarrow in 689. St. Peter's, Monkwearmouth, had been established in 674 at the mouth of the river Wear by Benedict Biscop. Jarrow is located in Northumbria, where the river Don flows into the Tyne. Bede tells us there were six hundred monks here in this (combined) monastery by the year 716. Both Jarrow and Monkwearmouth were abandoned in the ninth century after several Viking raids. *(Photo by Ray Beck. © St. Paul's Church, Jarrow.)*

and regarded as a single monastery. Both locations were under the same abbot.[50] Biscop died in 689 and was succeeded by Ceolfrith, who died in 716. Ceolfrith's letter is composed as a response to the Pictish king's request for advice about the keeping of Easter, the correct form of tonsure, and the Roman style in church architecture and other customs of the Roman Church. One can imagine Bede's delight at being asked to assist in offering advice of this sort! Also, there may have been internal strife within Pictland, and Nechtan may have seen this overture as an opportunity to promote unity and secure a political alliance of significant advantage. At the very beginning of the letter we note one of Bede's favorite allusions (already discussed above at V.9): a doctrinal reference to "citizens of our heavenly home, who are now pilgrims in this world," a linkage of heaven and earth by means of the concept of exile, temporary residence, and pilgrimage.

The major part of the letter of Ceolfrith to Nechtan next summarizes at great length the biblical, chronological, historical, and theological reasons that underlie the Roman position on the Easter controversy as generally understood and agreed in the English Church since the decision of Whitby in 664 (cf. III.25). The letter assumes the threefold scheme of Scriptural interpretation that is earlier found in such writers as Augustine of Hippo and Gregory the Great and which Bede had set forth in II.1: the literal or historical meaning, the allegorical or mystical meaning ("its bearing on the mysteries of Christ and the Church"), and the tropological or moral meaning. The letter then explains that the Roman position on the calculation of Easter as now officially held by the English Church, which it calls the "mystical reason" *(mystica ratio),* is the same as the second level of meaning spoken of by Gregory and Bede, which they call the allegorical or mystical, by which Christ is now no longer known merely as "promised before the law and under the law," but now, "with grace in the third dispensation of the world to be sacrificed for us as our Passover." Whoever disagrees with this catholic teaching about the date of Easter, the letter asserts, "disagrees with the teaching of the holy Scriptures in the celebration of the greatest mysteries, and agrees with those who trust that they can be saved without the grace

---

50. Bede also wrote the *History of the Abbots of Wearmouth and Jarrow,* ed. D. H. Farmer.

of Christ preventing [going before] them and who presume to teach that they could have attained to perfect righteousness even though the true Light had never conquered the darkness of the world by dying and rising again." There is also an indication of the depth of feeling and faith on this very central question that must have motivated persons like Ceolfrith and Bede: "So at last we duly celebrate our Easter feast to show that we are not, with the ancients, celebrating the throwing off of the yoke of Egyptian bondage but, with devout faith and love, venerating the redemption of the whole world, which, being prefigured by the liberation of the ancient people of God, is completed in the resurrection of Christ; we also signify that we rejoice in the sure and certain hope of our own resurrection, which we believe will also take place on a Sunday."

The letter also gives a passing credit to the earliest major historian of the worldwide church, Eusebius of Caesarea (who happens to be Bede's model historian) for his earlier work in the fourth century on the systematization of issues surrounding this question whereby yearly notifications of the correct date of Easter could be sent to other churches. Bede is obviously aware of the series of "festal letters," as they were called, that were distributed annually from the Patriarch of Alexandria. (They are also referenced in Eusebius' *Ecclesiastical History* VII.20-21.) Ceolfrith adds, however, that he himself does not propose to send information about future cycles and calculations, which is an ongoing process. (One may add, such discussions continue in ecumenical dialogues even today.)

After this exhausting excursus, the letter realistically concludes by observing that "we freely admit that a difference in tonsure is not hurtful to those whose faith in God is untainted and their love for their neighbor sincere." The letter seems to place the dispute over tonsure on a lower plane than the dispute over Easter, "especially since we never read that there was any conflict among the catholic fathers about differences of tonsure such as there has been about diversity in faith or in the keeping of Easter." Thus, in spite of some rather acrimonious disputes over forms of tonsure that Bede has earlier recorded (III.25, 26; IV.1), two reasons now seem to be given for placing it at a somewhat lower level of importance: 1) the earliest evidence about tonsure permits different conclusions, and 2) the tonsure dispute is a disciplinary controversy rather than a doctrinal one. As explained earlier, the Roman style of tonsure was a crown or circle of hair with the top shaven, and the Celtic style seems to have been only a half-crown shaven in the front, with hair growing at the top and back (although this interpretation is disputed). The claim that the Roman style of tonsure originated with St. Peter, as well as the attribution of the Celtic tonsure to Simon Magus, are both unhistorical.

Once the letter of Ceolfrith has been read aloud and translated in the presence of the king and his court, Nechtan, falling on his knees and thanking God, decrees that all the clergy and monks of his kingdom (cf. I.1, I.12, and IV.26) shall prefer the Roman, nineteen-year cycles for Easter calculation rather than the "erroneous" Celtic eighty-four-year cycles, and that they will adopt the circular, Roman tonsure. The transition from Celtic to Roman is thus accomplished in the kingdom of the Picts over the years 712-713.

Book V.22

The island and community of Iona finally accept the decision of Whitby in favor of the Roman dating for Easter and the Roman form of the tonsure in the year 716, under the influence of the holy monk Egbert, whose travels we have already encountered in III.27 and V.9. Because of the difficulties of translation explained at V.9, Egbert in V.9 and 22 seems to be erroneously labeled as a "bishop" in the Penguin (but not in the Oxford) translations, and also should not be confused with Archbishop Egbert of York who died in 766. The monk Egbert's death in 729 on the Roman, rather than the Celtic, date of Easter is taken by Bede as further proof that the Roman dating of Easter was truly God's design and that the Spirit is moving the Church from diversity to unity. Egbert has died on the very first day that Easter would have been celebrated at Iona on the basis of the Roman reckoning,[51] and only some two years before the time that Bede is writing.

51. April 24, whereas the latest date on the Celtic reckoning would have had to be April 21.

Book V.23

Tatwine succeeds Berhtwald as archbishop of Canterbury in 731. Some have suggested that the "two comets" mentioned here were probably one and the same, first approaching and then drawing away from the sun. There is much speculation, but no certainty, about the "swarm of Saracens" who ravaged Gaul, to whom Bede applies his formula of divine retribution. For a more negative judgment upon the England of his own day, made by Bede just a few years later and on the eve of his death, in which he laments the ignorance, neglect, and avarice that had become prevalent in the English Church, see his *Letter to Egbert* (734), appended to both the Oxford and Penguin translations. The chapter ends, finally, on a millenarian note. The future will show the result, and Bede, the historian, confesses his faith but declines to speculate.

Book V.24

Bede's concluding summary contains a number of uncorrected errors, and at times his chronology differs from the dates given earlier. The entry that begins with year 167 is entirely wrong, as was also the case in I.4, and corrections need to be made in the light of earlier comments at I.4. The summary in V.24 may have been written before, not after, the main body of Bede's text, and it contains occasional materials not included earlier. Surprising is the omission of the Synod of Whitby (664). Bede's concluding synopsis here, together with his Preface at the beginning, is about all we know concerning Bede's life and the titles of nearly all of the many works that he authored. Much of this has already been summarized above in the Introduction to this *Companion*. At the outset in his Preface, and again here in his concluding autobiographical note, both first and last, he describes himself as "servant of Christ and priest" *(famulus Christi et presbyter)*. The final word of the *History* is Bede's prayer, which could only have been written by a person who was both a scholar and a saint.

The following translation of Bede's prayer is offered by the present author of this *Companion:* "I pray you, Good Jesus, that as you have graciously permitted me to imbibe with joy the words of your knowledge, so also in your goodness you will grant me at length to come to yourself, the source of all Wisdom, and to remain in your presence for ever."

Some Questions for Subsequent Reflection

———⟨◦⟩———

1. What is Bede's own view of history? Does he reveal his purpose in writing this work? Is it millenarian? Is it a work of Christian apologetic? Does Bede have a Deuteronomic view, that is, does he believe that God is acting in history to reward those who are faithful? Is he consistent in this view, if, in fact he holds it at all?

2. How does Bede's treatment of the history of his own day differ from his handling of the history of earlier times? Do you agree with the view that he spends rather less space on the events of his own time because he is relatively displeased with what he regards as corruption that is overtaking much of the church's leadership?

3. Does Bede see the work of the church in England as a continuation of "sacred history" in his own day, much in the way that Eusebius back in the fourth century also saw the early patristic period as a continuation of the *Acts of the Apostles?*

4. Bede and miracles: Is Bede's status as a historian, in our post-Enlightenment scientific world, diminished by his belief in the miraculous? Are not some of the miracles that he records (e.g., in II.7 and V.2) capable of rational explanation? Is Bede more concerned with how miracles happened, or with their significance? Do accounts of miracles in Bede function analogously to the stories of persecution and martyrdom in Eusebius? What can we infer from the fact that Bede's usual word for "miracle" in the Latin text

is not *miraculum* (miracle) but *signum* (sign)? How often does Bede emphasize that the miracles he reports happened *in England*? Overall, how should one characterize Bede's attitude toward miracles: Are they for the purpose of the edification of other Christians? Are miracles a testimony to Christ? Perhaps a testimony to God's favor upon England? Or are Bede's miracles etiological explanations, invented to explain how things got to be the way they are? Or, conversely, is he recording natural events in which supernatural dimensions are revealed? Would he agree with the following definition given in the introduction to one of the Penguin editions: "A true miracle is not due to the supersession or inversion of the natural laws of the universe ordained by the Creator, but to the operation of cosmic laws as yet unrealized by man, activated by non-material forces whose potency is amply demonstrated in the Gospels"? Or would we be more likely to accept the explanation offered by Professor Deanesly: "Like his contemporaries, Bede believed that holiness of life and nearness to God might be attested by miraculous signs from heaven, either at the saint's prayer, or simply at the divine will. With this belief in the efficacious power of holiness went the firm belief in the saint's power after death, if prayer was made near his tomb, or even some object associated with him in life"?

5. Compare Bede's treatment of miracles with the handling they receive from the histories written by Godfrey, Deanesly, Mayr-Harting, or others. Which of these authors seems to treat miracles in a way closest to that of Bede himself? How would *you* classify and evaluate the miracles that Bede records? Why do so many modern histories of early England say almost nothing about his accounts of miracles but proceed to draw heavily upon Bede for almost everything else? The Introduction to one edition of the Penguin translation remarks that "It is clear that both sophisticated Romans and uncultured barbarians expected religion to be accompanied by miracles of one kind or another."

6. It is useful, when reading a classic work like Bede, to take notes on key topics that are mentioned in the text itself. Try doing this yourself, as you assess Bede's mentions and treatment of the following topics: Evangelism, Poverty, Daily Prayer, Bishops, Roman Church, Relics, Baptism, Preaching.

7. The decision of the 664 Synod of Whitby for Roman over Celtic Christianity (Book III.25) is obviously quite central for Bede. How does he contrast the Roman and the Celtic? Which side is he on? What do you make, for example, of his arguments presented to King Nechtan in Book V.21? How did geographical factors exaggerate, or perhaps even cause, the differences between the Celtic and Roman traditions of Christianity in early England? Which side would you have taken at Whitby and why?

8. If at some other time you happen to have read the *Ecclesiastical History* of Eusebius of Caesarea, how would you compare and contrast Bede with him? For example, does one or the other deal better or more fully with social, political, or economic factors? What is similar about their attitudes toward "history"? Do their respective treatments of the apostolic succession of bishops reveal anything about the political situation of the church in their times? What is the prevailing attitude toward "great men" in each of these histories; how is this attitude displayed in Eusebius' comments about a godly ruler and in Bede's presentation of a model bishop?

List of Popes from Gregory the Great

St. Gregory I (the Great)	590-604
Sabinian	604-606
Boniface III	607
St. Boniface IV	608-615
St. Deusdedit I	615-618
Boniface V	619-625
Honorius I	625-638
Severinus	640
John IV	640-642
Theodore I	642-649
St. Martin I	649-655
St. Eugene I	654-657
St. Vitalian	657-672
Deusdedit II	672-676
Donus	676-678
St. Agatho	678-681
St. Leo II	681-683
St. Benedict II	684-685
John V	685-686
Conon	686-687
St. Sergius I	687-701
John VI	701-705
John VII	705-707
Sisinnius	708

List of Popes from Gregory the Great

Constantine	708-715
St. Gregory II	715-731
St. Gregory III	731-741
St. Zachary	741-752

Source: *New Catholic Encyclopedia* (1967), vol. ii, p. 575.

Early Archbishops of Canterbury

―――⚬⚬⚬―――

1.	St. Augustine	597-604
2.	Laurence	604-619
3.	St. Mellitus	619-624
4.	St. Justus	624-627
5.	Honorius	627-653
6.	Deusdedit	655-664
7.	Theodore	668-690
8.	Berhtwald	693-731
9.	Tatwine	731-734
10.	Nothelm	735-739
11.	Cuthbert	740-760

Source: *Handbook of British Chronology,* ed. E. B. Fryde, D. E. Greenaway, S. Porter, and I. Roy (London: Royal Historical Society, 3rd edition, 1986), pp. 213-14.

James Campbell on the Significance of the Synod of Whitby [Bede III:25]

Bede makes it very clear that the calculation of the date of Easter was not a merely technical or isolated issue. The movement of Easter was one of many things which argument in terms of symbols (as we would say, but *symbol* is for us a limiting word, *mysteries* they would say) showed to be loaded with significance. Easter had to be just at the equinox, for the lengthening days represented Christ's triumph over the powers of darkness. It had to be in the first month of the lunar year, for this was the month in which the world had been created and in which it ought to be newly created. It had to be as the moon was about to wane, for the moon turns from earth toward the sun as it wanes, just as we should turn from earthly to heavenly things. It was appropriate that Easter should always fall within a space of seven days, for seven was a number of divine significance. Considered from another point of view, Easter was to be calculated in such a way as to fulfill both the Old Law of the Jews and the New Law of Christ. If it was celebrated at exactly the right time, then all was in harmony. Nothing can illustrate the gulf between Bede's thought-world and ours more vividly than his views on Easter. Such views were not simple popular piety. They formed part of an elaborate and not unsophisticated system of thought, which brought all knowledge into unity and to divine ends, and whose power depended on the capacity to see an allegory as a mysterious truth rather than as an illustration or a coincidence. Divergence between churches on such a matter as Easter was not a trivial matter. It was a rent in the seamless garment, and it is not surprising that Bede, who was by far the most learned man of his day on computation, would have devoted much of his history to this issue. . . .

Christ suffered at Passover, a feast which was celebrated at the first full moon of spring, and so was fixed by reference to a lunar calendar, and fell on varying dates within the solar year. Christians celebrated Easter at the same time, with this difference, that they came to hold the feast always on a Sunday, since Christ rose on that day. The Celtic churches calculated the date of Easter in accordance with rules which, although orthodox in the early fourth century, had later come to be regarded as unorthodox. The continental churches used more than one system of calculation; but they all differed from most of the Celts in important respects (though the southern Irish abandoned their old system shortly after 630). The most important was this. Both the Celts and their opponents agreed that Easter was to be calculated by reference to the full moon which came on or first after the spring equinox. But the Celts held Easter Sunday to be that which came in between the fourteenth day of the moon (i.e., the day of the full moon) and the twentieth, both included. That is to say, if the full moon came on a Sunday, they made this Easter Sunday. The other churches refused to make the day of the full moon Easter Sunday. Thus the system which Bede used, and which became universal in the west, reckoned Easter Sunday as that which fell between the fifteenth and the twenty-first days of the moon. If the full moon on or next after the equinox came on a Sunday, then the *next* Sunday was Easter Sunday.

There were other differences between the Celtic and the continental churches. The Celts made use of outmoded Easter cycles. (Because the solar year and the lunar month are constant, the date of Easter falls, not randomly, but in a sequence which is ultimately repeated; an Easter cycle is such a sequence, or part of one.) The Celts regarded the equinox as falling on March 25, while elsewhere the twenty-first was the accepted date — a divergence which could make a difference of twenty-eight days in the date of Easter.

Source: "Introduction" and "Notes" by James Campbell. Excerpted with permission of Washington Square Press/Pocket Books, an imprint of Simon & Schuster Adult Publishing Group from *Bede: The Ecclesiastical History of the English People,* edited, with Introduction by James Campbell, pp. xviii, 400-401. Copyright © 1968 by Simon & Schuster, Inc.

Bede: Table of Events 597-735
by James Campbell

Bede provides abundant dates in *The Ecclesiastical History*. He was a skilled chronologist, and it was largely thanks to him that the system of dating events from the birth of Christ came into general use. But the dates which he gives are not always consistent with one another, and there is uncertainty about the date on which he began the year (it was certainly not the first of January) and about other aspects of his reckoning. The subject is still controversial. The dates listed below are those which seem to me more probable....

597	Arrival of Augustine in Kent.
c.604	Mellitus becomes bishop of the East Saxons.
c.616	Death of Ethelbert, king of Kent.
c.616 or 617	Accession of Edwin as king of Northumbria.
c.617 or 618	Death of Saeberht, king of the East Saxons; they revert to paganism.
619 (?)	Paulinus sent to Northumbria.
627	Baptism of Edwin.
c.630	Accession of Sigeberht in East Anglia; Felix and Fursey arrive there not long afterwards.
633	Death of Edwin at the battle of Hatfield, where he is defeated by Penda, king of Mercia, and Cadwallon, king of Gwyned.
634	Battle of Heavenfield brings Oswald to power in Northumbria.
635	Aidan arrives in Northumbria from Iona.

c.635-638	Mission of Birinus to Wessex. Baptism of King Cynegils.
642	Battle of Maserfeld. Death of Oswald; succession of Oswy first to Bernicia and thereafter to the whole of Northumbria.
651	Death of Aidan.
653	Benedict Biscop's first journey to Rome.
653	Conversion of Paeda. Mission to the Middle Angles.
c.653	Cedd's mission to reconvert the East Saxons.
655	Battle on the Winwaed. Death of Penda of Mercia.
658	Wulfhere becomes king of Mercia after its rebellion against Oswy.
664	Synod of Whitby.
669	Theodore arrives in England to be archbishop of Canterbury.
672	Council of Hertford.
672 or 673	Birth of Bede.
674	Benedict Biscop founds the monastery of Wearmouth.
679	Council of Hatfield.
679 or 680	Bede enters the monastery of Wearmouth.
681-682	Benedict Biscop founds the monastery of Jarrow.
681-686	Wilfrid's conversion of Sussex.
690	Willibrord's mission to Frisia.
716	Iona accepts the Roman Easter.
731 or 732	Bede completes *The Ecclesiastical History*.
734	Bede's letter to Egbert.
735	Death of Bede.

Source: "Table of Events" by James Campbell. Excerpted with permission of Washington Square Press/Pocket Books, an imprint of Simon & Schuster Adult Publishing Group from *Bede: The Ecclesiastical History of the English People,* edited, with Introduction by James Campbell, pp. xxxix-xl. Copyright © 1968 by Simon & Schuster, Inc.

Select Bibliography and Suggestions for Further Reading

———⟨∞⟩———

As is remarked in the Introduction to this book, all quotations of Bede in this *Companion,* unless otherwise noted, are taken from the (latest) "Oxford World's Classics" 1999 paperback reissue of *Bede: The Ecclesiastical History of the English People,* edited by Judith McClure and Roger Collins and published by Oxford University Press, which is hereby recommended as being the version that is most useful and readily available. Another fine translation that can be followed with confidence is the latest revised (1990) "Penguin Classics" paperback, translated by Leo Sherley-Price and revised by R. E. Latham, with new introduction and notes by D. H. Farmer. This *Companion* can be easily used by readers of either the Oxford or Penguin editions. Those who wish to follow the Latin critical text, with facing English translation, are directed to Bertram Colgrave and R. A. B. Mynors, *Bede's Ecclesiastical History of the English People* in the Oxford Medieval Texts series (Oxford: Clarendon, first published in 1969). The translation found in the Oxford paperback edited by McClure and Collins is actually that of Colgrave and Mynors, but improved with corrections. Prepared to accompany the scholarly Latin text of McClure and Collins, and also quite scholarly in content, is J. M. Wallace-Hadrill, *Bede's Ecclesiastical History: A Historical Commentary,* Oxford Medieval Texts (Oxford: Clarendon, 1988). An older translation, which itself builds upon its predecessors and is still useful at some points, is *Bede: The Ecclesiastical History of the English People and Other Selections,* edited by James Campbell (New York: Washington Square Press, 1968). It should also be noted that the earliest general history of the Christian Church, by Eusebius of Caesarea, in English translation by G. A. Williamson, is published by Penguin in various editions at various dates.

There are four fine histories of the English Church of Bede's day published within the last half-century: Margaret Deanesly, *The Pre-Conquest Church in England* (London: Adam & Charles Black, 1961; 2nd edition 1963); C. J. Godfrey, *The Church in Anglo-Saxon England* (Cambridge: Cambridge University Press, 1962); Henry Mayr-Harting, *The Coming of Christianity to Anglo-Saxon England* (University Park: Pennsylvania State University Press, 1972; 3rd edition 1991); and John Blair, *The Church in Anglo-Saxon Society* (Oxford: Oxford University Press, 2005). For the overall sweep of English Church history at a very fundamental and elementary level, distilling the essence of the period that Bede dealt with and then moving on up into the last century, the first thirty or forty pages of J. R. H. Moorman, *A History of the Church in England* (London: Adam and Charles Black, 1980), can still be read with profit. There is also a plethora of fine secondary articles and books on Bede and related subjects, of which the entry on Bede in the new *Oxford Dictionary of National Biography,* ed. H. C. G. Matthew and Brian Harrison (Oxford: Oxford University Press, 2004), is outstanding. The following volumes are also especially noteworthy:

Clinton Albertson, ed., *Anglo-Saxon Saints and Heroes* (New York: Fordham University Press, 1967).

C. J. Arnold, *An Archaeology of the Early Anglo-Saxon Kingdoms* (London: Routledge, 1997).

C. F. Battiscombe, ed., *The Relics of St. Cuthbert* (London: Oxford University Press, 1956).

P. H. Blair, *The World of Bede* (Cambridge: Cambridge University Press, 1970, rev. 1990).

G. Bonner, ed., *Famulus Christi: Essays in Commemoration of the Thirteenth Century of the Birth of the Venerable Bede* (London: Society for Promoting Christian Knowledge, 1976).

N. Brooks, *The Early History of the Church of Canterbury* (Leicester: Leicester University Press, 1984).

Gerald M. Browne, trans., *The Abbreviated Psalter of the Venerable Bede* (Grand Rapids: Eerdmans, 2002).

J. Campbell, ed., *The Anglo-Saxons* (Oxford: Phaedon, 1982).

————, *Essays in Anglo-Saxon History* (London: Hambledon, 1986).

Caitlin Corning, *The Celtic and Roman Traditions: Conflict and Consensus in the Early Medieval Church* (New York: Palgrave Macmillan, 2006).

Margaret Deanesly, *Sidelights on the Anglo-Saxon Church* (London: Black, 1962).

Scott DeGregorio, ed., *Innovation and Tradition in the Writings of the Venerable Bede* (Morgantown: West Virginia University Press, 2006).

D. H. Farmer, ed., *The Age of Bede* (Harmondsworth: Penguin, 1988) [Includes translations of Bede's *Life of Cuthbert* and *Lives of the Abbots,* as well as of *The Voyage of St Brendan* and of Eddius's *Life of Wilfrid*].

Marion J. Hatchett, "The Eucharistic Rite of the Stowe Missal," pp. 153-70 of *Time and Community: In Honor of Thomas Julian Talley,* ed. J. Neil Alexander (Washington, D.C.: The Pastoral Press, 1990).

N. J. Higham, *(Re-)Reading Bede* (New York: Routledge, 2006).

S. Hollis, *Anglo-Saxon Women and the Church* (Woodbridge, U.K.: Boydell, 1992).

E. James, "Bede and the Tonsure Question," *Peritia* 3 (1984): 85-98.

D. P. Kirby, *The Earliest English Kings* (London: Routledge, 1992).

W. Levison, *England and the Continent in the Eighth Century* (Oxford: Oxford University Press, 1956).

Daniel McCarthy, "On the Shape of the Insular Tonsure," *Celtica* 24 (2003): 140-67.

W. D. McCready, *Miracles and the Venerable Bede* (Toronto: Pontifical Institute of Medieval Studies, 1994).

J. L. G. Meissner, *The Celtic Church in England After the Synod of Whitby* (London: Hopkinson, 1929).

S. J. Ridyard, *The Royal Saints of Anglo-Saxon England* (Cambridge: Cambridge University Press, 1988).

David Rollason, *Saints and Relics in Anglo-Saxon England* (Oxford: Blackwell, 1989).

F. M. Stenton, *Anglo-Saxon England* (Oxford: Oxford University Press, 1965).

M. Swanton, *The Dream of the Rood* (Manchester: Manchester University Press, 1970).

H. M. and J. Taylor, *Anglo-Saxon Architecture*, 3 vols. (Cambridge: Cambridge University Press, 1965-78).

Alan Thacker and Richard Sharpe, eds., *Local Saints and Local Churches in the Early Medieval West* (Oxford: Oxford University Press, 2002).

Charles Thomas, *Christianity in Roman Britain to A.D. 500* (London: Batsford, 1981).

A. H. Thompson, ed., *Bede: His Life, Times and Writings* (Oxford: Oxford University Press, 1935).

Benedicta Ward, *The Venerable Bede* (Kalamazoo, Mich.: Cistercian Publications, 1998).

J. F. Webb, ed. and trans., *Lives of the Saints* (Baltimore: Penguin, 1965).

L. Webster and J. Backhouse, eds., *The Making of England: Anglo-Saxon Art and Culture AD 600-900* (London: British Museum Press, 1991).

D. M. Wilson, ed., *The Archaeology of Anglo-Saxon England* (London: Methuen, 1976).

B. Yorke, *Kings and Kingdoms of Early Anglo-Saxon England* (London: Routledge, 1990).

In addition, the bibliographical compendiums of Wilfrid Bonser, *An Anglo-Saxon and Celtic Bibliography 450-1087*, 2 vols. (1957), and W. F. Bolton, "A Bede Bibliography 1935-1960," *Traditio* xviii (1962): 436-45 are still very useful. Reference works that should be noted include C. R. Cheney, ed., *A Handbook of Dates for Students of British History*, Royal Historical Society Guides and Handbooks no. 4; new edition revised by Michael Jones (Cambridge and New York: Cambridge University Press, 2000); D. Hill, *An Atlas of Anglo-Saxon England* (Oxford: Blackwell, 1981); and *Handbook of British Chronology*, ed. E. B. Fryde, D. E. Greenaway, S. Porter, and I. Roy (London: Royal Historical Society, 3rd edition, 1986).

Index

Aaron, 19

Abbot John. *See* John (abbot)

Abgar IX (king of Edessa), 15

Absolution, 104; and penance, 106

Acca (bishop of Hexham), 69-70, 122

Adamnan (abbot of Iona), 119-120

Adamnan (Irish monk), 106

Addi, 113

Adomnan. *See* Adamnan (abbot of Iona)

Aebbe, 106

Aesica, 96

Aethelburh, 96

Aethelthryth. *See* Etheldreda

Agatho (Pope): on monotheletism, 100; Wilfrid's appeal to, 121

Aidan, 8, 60; Bede's evaluation of, 73; bones of, 111; death of, 71, 72-73; and Hilda, 105; ministry of, 62-63; miracles of, 71-73; as model bishop, 29, 64-65; and Oswine, 70-71

Aidan's Pillar, 72-73

Alban, 16-19

Albinus, 12

Albion. *See* Britain

Aldhelm, 120

Aldred, 108

Alleluia, 24

Altar, 54; of idols and Christians, 18; at

places of worship, 38-39; as portable, 117; on Raedwald, 56

Ambrose, 30

Amphibalus, 16-18

Anatolius, 62

Andrew: and archbishop of Canterbury, 89; monastery of, 25

Angles, 24. *See also* Anglo-Saxons

Anglicans: on Bede, 5; on Synod of Whitby, 83-84

Anglo-Saxons, 14; and Britons, 21; and Celts, 59

Anno ab incarnatione Domini, 2

Anno dominicae incarnationis, 2

Antoninus, 17

Apostasy, 67-68

Apostles' Creed, 3

Arculf, 119

Arianism, 19

Armagh, 84

Ascension, 8

Asterius, 66

Athanasius, 52, 74

Audrey. *See* Etheldreda

Augustine of Canterbury: as archbishop of Britain, 46; and Christ Church, 40; and conversion of Ethelbert, 30-31; death of, 47; and Gregorian mission to Britain, 25-29; and Gregory the Great,